D1596802

1-2010

John,

I thought you would
enjoy this read.
It's a little piece
of Jacksonville
entrepreneurial
History -

Rob

Newboy

The Autobiography of

Herbert Hill Peyton

First printing - 1997
Second printing - 2007

Library of Congress Catalog Card Number: 97-091993

International Standard Book Number: 0-9658277-0-4

Gate Petroleum Company
9540 San Jose Boulevard
Jacksonville, Florida 32257

Composition and design by Husk Jennings, Jacksonville, Florida

*Printed in the United States of America
by Edwards Brothers, Inc. Lillington, North Carolina*

Dedication

This book is dedicated to the Gate Brothers and Sisters,
who started with so little and came so far.

Contents

Prologue

Have you ever wondered what evidence of your life might remain one hundred years from now?

I have written this book because one hundred years from now there probably will be no other trace that I have lived on earth. Our great-grandchildren most likely will not know our names; they will have minimal interest in our having lived, or in what we did during our stay on this earth.

I share everyone's secret desire to leave his mark when he dies, whether it be through material things, or memories, or relationships with other people...something that sets him apart and makes him unique from the millions off souls who come into this world without their consent and leave against their will.

Because of my transient upbringing, I matured very late in some areas of my life, and in other areas it was necessary to mature at a very early age. Time has a way of editing the bad memories from your life. However, I well remember that in those early years loneliness was always with me or close at hand.

Almost half of the original Gate brothers have already died. If these stories of long ago days in Kentucky and the early days of Gate are not told now, they will be lost forever.

I will now tell you the story of Newboy.

Herbert Hill Peyton

Preface

"Read history and works of truth, not novels and romances...never touch a novel. They print beauty more charming than nature, and describe happiness that never exists. They will teach (one) to sigh after that which has no reality, to despise the little good that is granted us in this world and to expect more than is given."

General Robert E. Lee

General Lee's observations about books are correct. Reality is an extraordinary teacher. I am qualified to tell you the story of Newboy because I have lived this adventure.

The success of Gate had to have been the result of a combination of being at the right place at the right time, and being able to assemble the management team to take advantage of these unique circumstances; and above all, there had to be a helluva lot of luck all along the way.

Most military campaigns succeed or fail because of these same factors. I have read many of the books written about the military history of this country. D-Day in Europe, June 6, 1944, was without doubt the biggest day of the century in the military history of the United States. It was a tremendous undertaking and has got to be the high water mark.

I was twelve years old, carrying newspapers in Kentucky, when Eisenhower went out to talk to the paratroopers on the eve of D-Day. I saw that photograph on the front page of our paper. Seeing those men all ready to go made a tremendous impression on me, and I decided right then and there I wanted to be in the paratroopers. I also was really sorry that I missed Normandy. I was about six years too young.

In the last century, the Battle of Gettysburg was one of the seven most decisive battles in the history of the world. It was important because if the South had won at Gettysburg, Lincoln would probably have sued for peace and we probably would have two countries today. The fascinating, unbelievable thing about the Civil War was that the South was outmanned and outgunned and the North had all the arms factories and resources. Yet the South was able to win just about every major battle, because of the quality of the Confederate soldiers and their generals.

I visited Gettysburg, and have always thought that the battle fought there provided a classic example of an individual — General Lee — so successful in all his military strategies and battles, that after awhile he thought his troops could do anything.

Lee had always relied on Stonewall Jackson for advice and support. If Jackson had not been killed at Chancellorsville, I don't think Gettysburg would ever have happened. But Lee had achieved so much during his campaign in northern Virginia that without Jackson to warn him, he began to think his army was invincible. Lee tried to cross that mile-wide open field with 15,000 men. The Yankees were dug in behind the rock wall on Cemetery Ridge, and it couldn't be done.

I have seen that happen many times in business and in life when, because a man has been successful, he thinks he can do anything; and therein lies serious trouble.

I've always been a student of military history, and I've always equated Gate to a military campaign. We have fought many battles.

Acknowledgements

I can assure those of you who have never written a book that it is not an easy task. Without the perseverance and guidance of my longtime Mandarin friend Gini Barker, this book would not have been possible. Thank you, Gini.

Friends have played an important part in my life. Without my friend Dave Clavier helping me take this book the last mile we never would have reached the finish line.

—Part One—

— Chapter One —

Traipsin'

We scuffled our toes in the hot Kentucky dust of the schoolyard while two captains chose sides for the first softball game of September. Only the faces and the fenced field were different from the fall before, and from the fall before that. I was a new student as usual, at an unfamiliar school, watching an otherwise familiar back-to-school ceremony: team captains calling names to split a gaggle of schoolboys, in the local pecking order of descending desirability, into teams. When even the least wanted had been chosen and I stood alone on the bare infield, I heard the inevitable, reluctant last line: "Well, okay, I'll take Newboy."

The scene was too familiar to be painful. I had attended a different Kentucky or Tennessee school each September for as long as I could remember, and simply expected to make—even fight—my way up from last place in each new schoolyard.

Even in my earliest memory, our family is on the move, jouncing up a rocky dry creekbed in a black two-door '36 Ford sedan, on the way to a remote lumber camp—Mother, Pa, Brother, Sister, and me. I was about four years old, and I remember standing up in the back seat of that Ford, with groceries around me, and getting carsick from riding in that rough creekbed, the only way in. It was six miles up there, Brother says. I don't remember, but it took a hell of a long time. After you got in there, they had dirt roads.

I was born in Bowling Green, Kentucky, January 6, 1932, and we had moved around Kentucky those early years. My father had grown up in Charlottesville, Virginia, and had quit high school when he was a sophomore. He met my mother in New York, where he had a construction job. Mother had grown up in Bowling Green, where her father was a lawyer, and she had gone to Randolph-Macon College and to art school before going to work in New York.

Mother and Pa got married in New York when my father was about twenty-five, and they moved all over the country. They lived in Chicago; then in Berkeley, California, where Brother was born; then went back to New York; and after they'd been married for several years, wound up in Bowling Green without a job, in the middle of the Depression. Pa had been given a year's leave of absence without pay, and they lived with my mother's father.

Then Pa went to work for Ches Wyman Company, in the lumber business, and we moved to Louisville, their headquarters, where Pa worked at the lumber mill. Later he cruised timber for trees eventually to be cut into barrel staves for the whiskey business.

We lived in some very remote places, like Cumberland Falls, Tennessee; and Somerset and Buckhorn and Hindman, Kentucky. Buckhorn, with no road in but the rough creekbed I remember so clearly, had no electric lights and no plumbing; we had kerosene lanterns and an outhouse. Most of the people up there were mountaineers. We didn't live there very long. We didn't live anywhere very long.

My brother, Gaines Peyton, is two-and-a-half years older than I am, and my sister, Sally, is three years younger.

My brother and I moved and changed schools every year, so we stuck together all through our childhood. We went everywhere together and were closer than most brothers. And we had many good times.

When I was six years old, Pa had gone to work for Spur Oil in Bowling Green, and I began first grade there. I remember my teacher had taught my mother in the first grade, and she expected me to be a great artist like my mother.

My first day of school, she called me into the cloakroom and asked me to paint her something, and I had zero talent. She was quite shocked, because my mother was a fine artist. Mother painted oil portraits and had quite a reputation throughout Kentucky, having painted portraits of many of the leading citizens of that area.

I remember Pa in his Spur Oil uniform. After several weeks of training in Bowling Green he was transferred to the home office in Nashville to be in charge of construction of service stations, so in the summer between my first and second grade, we moved back to Tennessee. We lived in four different homes in Nashville in five years, and I changed schools every year. If Pa didn't move from town to town, he would move around in the same town. Pa always moved, all his life.

Brother was three years ahead of me in school. We did have some fights with the neighbors, but we usually worked it out, after awhile. I was skinny and little, and each time I began as Newboy in a new school, I had to cope with bullies at recess and when school was out. I instinctively knew never to show any apprehension or concern or emotion when confronted by someone who wanted to whip me.

I did get in fights at school on occasion, and I did get whipped on occasion, but even then, the bullies never wanted to fight me again because they knew it was going to be harder than they had anticipated and that I did not respond to threats, which they found very frustrating.

I remember being tested by a class bully when I was in the fourth grade. On one of the very first days of school, we were up on a mezzanine balcony in the library and this big boy said, "We ought to throw Newboy off this balcony." I guess I was supposed to show great fear and beg him not to do it. Several boys were there, all bigger than I was.

Even at that early age of ten, I said, "That's a pretty good idea, but I'll tell you one thing. Whoever does the throwing is going to go with me," and they got out of the notion. I didn't ever attempt to run; I never showed intimidation; and I think that is a behavior that served me well in later life.

The result of this personality development is what I call Newboy training. Newboy training on the surface meant being quiet to avoid attention. It was actually much deeper than that, and it involved a whole mode of behavior. Newboy training never permitted me to show any emotion: no crying, no excitement, no disappointment; and never allowed me to show any signs of being startled or surprised.

This behavior was dictated not only by a physical fear of getting whipped, but also by a fear of not being accepted in the unfamiliar, unfriendly, constantly changing environments.

Although as I grew older, it was easier for me to fit into new groups, the basic Newboy training has stayed with me all my life, and affects my personality even today.

While we lived in Nashville, in second grade I went to Stokes, in third grade to Palmer, fourth grade to Robinson Academy, fifth grade to David Lipscomb, and sixth grade to Donelson.

The first place we lived was Observatory Drive, and then we moved to my favorite place in Nashville, Granny White Pike. When we moved to Granny White Pike, Pa took us out there, which was about fifteen miles from Nashville. And then he left in the only car we had, a '39 Ford, for three weeks.

My mother and her three children were out in the country with no way to get to the grocery store — or anywhere, for that matter — and in a remote area where we knew nobody. How Mother got by out there I never have understood completely, but she seemed to get by.

Pa was pretty slick to convince my mother during those lean years that she should go five years without a new dress while he had to be dressed in a suit at all times, because it was necessary to make a good impression in business.

He paid $2,500 for that place on Granny White Pike: two acres and an old white one-story frame house, with screened front and back porches. The only means of heating was a coal fireplace in every room. During the winter, I remember we shut off most of the house and lived in two or three rooms. There were fireplaces in the kitchen, living room, dining room, and two bedrooms in the main part of the house. My brother and I had a bedroom off the back porch, with no heat at all. I can remember a few blizzards when it would be below zero, and we slept back there with about a foot of blankets on the bed.

My job was to get up every morning, about five o'clock, and carry in the coal. Pa's job was to stand on the hearth in his wool suit and holler for the coal.

The house was on a very steep hill, right next door to a blacksmith. We planted a garden on the side of that hill, but after a hard spring rain all the seed wound up in the bottom of the ditch. Brother claimed that he didn't have adequate tools, and what he really needed was a mule and a plow to work that garden. Pa used to get us the cheapest spade and hoe that you could buy, and when one of these tools hit that hard Tennessee clay, it would bounce.

In spite of all that, the whole family loved Granny White Pike, and it was our favorite home.

We had moved to Granny White Pike in the summer, and I can clearly remember having a discussion at the supper table one night about what school we would go to and how we would go about getting registered.

Pa had a very simple solution for that, as he did for most things. He said, "Get down there beside the road, and catch the first school bus that comes by." And we did. Brother and I wound up at the wrong school, and we got off the bus and walked in just like we belonged there, went into the first available classroom, and sat down. They called the roll, and we knew we didn't belong there—so we just sat there and listened. When they found that we were extra students, they called us to the office of the principal and she arranged to have a car take us to the proper school.

The proper school was Palmer, where I went to the third grade. I remember, one day after I had been there about two months, I was throwing paper in the lunch room. I didn't know it, but the principal, Mrs. Talley, was standing right back of me. She grabbed me by both arms and shook me like a rag doll, until my teeth rattled. And she yelled at me in a shrill voice, "We have had nothing but trouble since you and your brother came here, and I'm not putting up with it any more!"

She then stopped shaking me, and I was supposed to cry or say I was sorry, or something of that sort. But she didn't know about Newboy training. I just looked her in the eye and asked her, "What time is it?" Then she had a big time fit, and she marched me off to the office. She intensely disliked me from then on.

Pa had bought the '39 Ford in 1940. A dark blue, four-door sedan, it was a good-looking car. Pa claimed it was new, but it wasn't; Brother and I knew he bought it from a man in New York, and it had been in storage for about a year. But it was like new, and as I recall, he paid $800 for it — the nicest car Pa ever had. We kept it for a long time.

I remember about that time we decided to go to Virginia in that Ford, to visit Pa's family for Christmas. The back door on the '39 Fords was hinged on the back and opened at the front, and this caused trouble on that trip.

The car had a heater in the front, but Brother and I were in the back seat where it was cold, so we had blankets to cover our feet. Pa was going about sixty miles an hour. Brother's blanket got stuck in the back door, so he opened the door to get the blanket loose and the door was jerked out of his hand, hit the back fender, and sprung the hinge.

Pa stopped the car, got out, walked around; he looked at the door, he looked at Brother, and he said, "God damn you, Genz!" Brother's first name is Gaines, which was my Mother's maiden name, but because of Pa's Virginia accent, he couldn't pronounce Gaines and always called him "Genz." Pa got back in the car and we proceeded to Virginia.

Granny White Pike was a real rough neighborhood, and we ran with some tough boys out there. One of the families was named Tomlinson; one was Shoats (which was a very appropriate name). The Shoats had a very efficient garbage disposal plan in their house. They had a hole in their kitchen floor, and they'd sweep all the garbage through the hole. Their hogs were everywhere— they ran loose in the yard—and they came under the house to get the garbage.

To go anywhere at Granny White Pike was a long walk or bike ride. One time Brother and I and a couple of other boys were walking across a big pasture; I must have been about nine, in the third grade. We turned around and saw this bull charging us wide open with his horns down. We took off running, but it was a long way to the fence. The other boys were bigger than I was, and I couldn't keep up.

I looked around and the bull was about fifteen yards in back of me and closing fast. Brother was concerned, but nevertheless, he was about ten yards in front of me. As he ran, he was watching over his shoulder to see what was going to happen.

I went down with one clean swoop and picked up a rock about the size of a golf ball, and turned around and threw that rock just as hard as I could; hit that bull dead between the eyes—and he stopped dead in his tracks. Brother was amazed that I had the presence of mind to do that, and he told about it with great pride.

While we lived at Granny White Pike, Brother always had a pet or two. One time he kept a baby owl on our screened-in back porch. Another time, we went blackberry picking in the spring and found a skunk hole. We dug up the hole and got six baby skunks, and had a pet skunk for some time. But that didn't work out very well because the skunk would bite. Pa didn't like the skunk, and the skunk didn't like Pa.

Brother was an authority on hawks and could tell what kind they were at a glance, but he didn't like crows. He spent most of his youth pursuing crows. He had a thing about crows, and when a crow would caw, it would set Brother crazy trying to find out where he was so he could get a bead on him. I can remember one time a friend of ours told me that Brother had come to his house and waked him up at daylight; said there were crows, he could hear them cawing. This friend said hell, Brother had already ridden his bike six miles to get over there after those crows, and it was just barely daylight.

As we moved all over Nashville, Brother developed another ritual. As we drove to a new home, you could see him looking out the car windows for the creeks. In each new neighborhood, the first thing he would do was get on his bike and start scouting to locate all the creeks and nearby rivers, and that's where he would spend the bulk of his time. He was at home there; he knew every crook and turn of every damn creek within five miles of each place we lived in Nashville. He knew every river, what kinds of fish were there, and how to catch them. Brother became quite an outdoorsman during that period in Nashville. We spent a good deal of our time on the creeks fishing, hunting in the woods, and camping.

About a mile beyond our Granny White Pike house was a really big creek called the Little Harpeth River. We used to go rockfishing, or grappling. That is, we would wade up and down that creek for miles; and up there, you would have these banks with overhangs, and you'd feel up under the banks and rocks with your hands for fish. Brother would just reach back under rocks and whatever was there, he would grab. Brother's mission was to catch fish, but he came out sometimes with turtles or crawfish or whatever was back there. That sport never did excite me much, but that was Brother's idea of how to spend the day, grappling.

Brother and I were very close friends, but Sister, being younger, kind of ran in a separate group. Mother was always promoting Sister to us. She told us that Sister was remarkable and Sister was wonderful. I never heard Brother referred to as remarkable; he never did claim that he was. We didn't see much of Sister, but Mother looked out after her—you could always count on that. Sister didn't do so well on the grappling, or the crow hunting.

You would think Brother wasn't paying much attention sometimes, but Brother had a way of watching everything pretty close. I remember we used to have an electric toaster that sat on the table at breakfast, and right before it would pop up, it would make a little clicking noise, you barely could hear it if you listened real close. But Brother could hear it, and he'd grab that toast. From the time he would hear that clicking he had it timed perfectly, so he'd have his hand there, and when the toast jumped up a few seconds later, he knew exactly when to put out his hand, all in one motion, and he never missed a piece of toast.

Mother decided that we should move away from Granny White Pike. She convinced Pa that the neighborhood and the boys we ran with were too rough, and not a very good influence on us. Brother and I agreed they were rather country, but they were good people. Anyway, my parents decided they were not up to our standards, and we should move.

When Pa was trying to sell the Granny White Pike house, Brother and I didn't want to move. I remember one time some prospective buyers came by, and Brother was sitting on a log in the back yard. They were asking Brother all about the house. Brother was not too enthusiastic in his sales pitch, and he told them the well went dry in summer.

Pa heard about that and raised hell. The well did go dry in summer, but Pa didn't want to tell it. And the prospective buyers never came back. But we eventually did sell the house and move back closer to town, to Caldwell Lane.

Caldwell Lane was across town—we changed schools again—and had a nice two-story brick house on about an acre of land. Brother and I had the job of cutting the grass; and understand, back in those days there was no motor on the lawnmower, it was strictly push. Pa bought the cheapest push mower available.

I remember when Pa would go on a trip and say, "When I get back, I want all this grass cut." And we'd have a helluva time keeping up with that grass. It'd get ahead of us, and get tall, and the damn cheap lawnmower wouldn't cut it. Pa convinced Brother that if he pushed that lawnmower it would develop his shoulders and help him play football. Pa'd come back off a trip, and if the grass was tall, he'd raise hell. Brother would tell him, "Well, it's been raining every day and we couldn't cut the grass in the rain." I don't know whether or not the lawnmower made Brother strong, but he did grow up and play football on the Robinson Academy team, and was a good athlete.

Years later when we'd moved—and we'd always

move—I remember running into some of the boys he'd gone to Robinson Academy with. They'd lost track of us and told me they'd watched all the football rosters of the Southeast Conference after we moved, because they thought Brother would be playing for some Southeast Conference football team, for sure.

When Brother was in the eighth grade he was bigger than anybody in the school. He looked somewhat like Lil' Abner—he was really muscled-up and had a very small waist and broad shoulders. Then he quit growing at about fourteen or fifteen years old, and wound up about the size I eventually got to be—about five-feet-ten and 150 pounds.

When I was in the fourth grade, I played on the Robinson Academy football team. Brother and I joined the Boy Scout troop there, Troop #1, and he was a very active Scout. I was too young, but I went to the meetings. They were real informal—we played basketball and football. We had a Scoutmaster named Billy Jim. He was much of a man and spent a lot of time with us, and we thought he was about as good as you could do.

Robinson Academy was a public school but had been named many years before, when it was a private academy. For the fifth grade, although we still lived at Caldwell Lane, I changed schools and went to David Lipscomb.

As far as my scholastic ability went, I didn't do so hot. I always passed. I never flunked a course in grammar school, high school, or college, but I always had to struggle, and I never made the Honor Roll.

The issue to me was very simple. You either passed or you didn't pass. That was the name of the game, and I used all methods to pass. No holds barred. The last few days before exams, I was very desperate, and I learned early to get the smartest students to tutor me. I worried them to death, including getting them up early in the morning to beat answers into my head before the exam. I learned early that I could be super friendly to the teachers, and convey to them my interest and very sincere efforts to study and learn. I was also quiet, which they liked.

While we lived at Caldwell Lane, Brother and I had a typical encounter with my mother's sister, Hallie Fisher. She was a favorite relative of mine, a college professor from Bristol, Virginia, and a real supporter of the Peyton family who visited us wherever we lived, nearly every summer. On this occasion, Hallie was visiting at the same time housepainters were working at our house. Brother and I put the painters' ladder up to our second floor bedroom window one night and went out the window.

We went up to a nearby highway, the Franklin Pike, in the rain, and started making mudballs and throwing them at cars. We were on a bank above the highway, and these real hard mudballs would damn near knock them off the road when they hit. One car stopped and the driver got out and started chasing us. It was pitch black out there, and that sonofabitch chased us all over the neighborhood. Finally, we got scared and ran up the ladder into the bedroom and pushed the ladder back over so he couldn't come up. He thought he saw us come up there and go into the house, but he wasn't sure.

He knocked on the front door, and when Mother answered, he said, "Your boys have been outside throwing mudballs at my car and almost caused me to have a wreck." Hallie was there, and took charge of the situation immediately. She went upstairs to see if we were there. We had mud all over us, and had gotten in the beds and pulled the sheets up and were pretending to be sleeping. Hallie turned on the light and there was mud all over the room. She could see the mud through the sheets. She called back down the stairs to Mother, waiting at the front door with the man, who was mad as hell, "No, I'm sorry, it couldn't be these boys. These boys are up here sleeping," and the man left. Later we got threats and a lecture from Hallie and Mother.

We had a pretty good time at Caldwell Lane. Robinson Academy was a good school, and we did well. But Pa had a chance to get a good price for the Caldwell Lane house in the midst of the World War II housing shortage, so we sold and moved way out east of Nashville in the country.

In Tennessee, we moved not only around Nashville, but around the entire Davidson County. I remember moving was always quite a tough day. We hauled everything in trucks and in Pa's car. Now Pa was always proud of his car. He had the '36 Ford, the '39, and then he got a '41 Ford. The one he was most proud of was a '42 Pontiac, a company car. We moved from Caldwell Lane to Donelson in that Pontiac.

Brother was always very protective of his steel traps. Brother ran a trapline at all times, everywhere we lived. When we moved into a new neighborhood, one of his rituals before we even got settled, the first thing, was to set out his trapline around the surrounding territory. He'd catch whatever was there: possums, 'coons, skunks, groundhogs and foxes. But Brother never entrusted his steel traps to the movers.

I can remember him hauling about twenty steel traps into the back seat of Pa's Pontiac. And Pa said, "Get those goddam traps out of my car and leave them!" But Brother didn't leave them; he took them everywhere he went.

Back then there was a market for hides. You could get two dollars for a skunk, three or four dollars for a 'coon, and at least ten dollars for a fox fur.

We rented a farm with a one-story frame house at Donelson. The Storeys, who owned the farm, had goats and chickens, mules and cows, and lived in a tenant house some distance in back of the farm house. I can remember on one of our first days there, Mother was hanging up the wash and she looked around and saw a goat charging her with its horns down. She screamed and ran in the house.

When the Storeys were out of town, Brother and I would milk the cows and do chores for them. Come cow milking time, Mr. Storey had a little trick. He would put out a little feed, just enough to get the cows to put their heads in the stalls; then he'd lock their heads in with these little slats and they'd be trapped there until milking was through.

The chickens used to look at us through the back screen door while we were eating. We lived out there for the usual period of time, which was one year. Brother and I spent a good deal of time on the nearby Cumberland River. We both went to Donelson schools. I was Newboy, in sixth grade. Brother was a freshman in high school, and went out for the football team. He did pretty well; he didn't make the first team but he got to play some.

As we moved around Nashville, we lived near orphanages more than once. We could always go up the road to the orphans' home and get up a football game. We played tackle football with two-man teams, and Brother and I played as a team. We'd go knock on the door and say, "We want two volunteers out here for a game of football."

We would see them looking out the windows while Brother and I warmed up in the yard. After awhile, two of the toughest orphans would run out to accept the challenge.

Orphans played dirty. We'd always have to tell them, prior to the game, "Alright now, we don't want any neck wringing, and no jumping on a downed player with your knees."

Our family grew to love Nashville. It was a great town to live in, and although I was "Newboy" in a different school every year, those were good years. Pa was traveling a lot, but Mother was always home—we did fine.

— Chapter Two —

Bowling Green, Kentucky

In the summer after my sixth grade year, we moved back to Bowling Green, Kentucky. It seemed like we always moved in the summer. Pa was still working in Nashville and drove the sixty-five miles home each Friday in his '42 Pontiac. We lived at the same place we'd always lived in Bowling Green, a duplex owned by mother's father, at 1220 State Street. We lived in the upstairs apartment; the house was on a main street three blocks from the square.

Bowling Green was a town of about 14,000 people. It was the county seat of Warren County and the home of Western Kentucky University, and it was a nice town. I attended Bowling Green Junior High School and began high school there, and today when people ask me where I'm from, I tell them without thinking, "Bowling Green," which I've always considered home. Brother and I stayed for the next four years.

My mother's father, Walter Gaines, was a lawyer in Bowling Green. As a young man, after graduation from the University of Kentucky law school, he was en route somewhere to practice law and his train stopped at Bowling Green. During the layover he got off the train and walked down to town, decided he liked it there, and stayed all his life.

He married a Bowling Green girl, and as a result, we were kin to quite a few people there, like the Hineses and the Helmses, and knew most of the Bowling Green families.

Our friends were close friends and just the finest people you could imagine. I have kept up with some of these folks over the years.

The only person of any halfway celebrity from Bowling Green was Duncan Hines, the famous food man who endorsed restaurants "Recommended by Duncan Hines." We claimed kinship to him, but he didn't claim us.

My grandfather's house had a very small back yard and front yard, and we lived next door to the Coca-Cola franchisee. Bowling Green was a farming community, and the only people who had money in that town were the doctors, the bankers, and of course, the Coca-Cola franchisee.

Of course, the business of a Coca-Cola franchisee was the sale of sweetened water. Brother and I never indulged in colas or similar drinks which we referred to as a belly wash, it was contrary to our athletic ambitions. You see, Brother and I were in full athletic training even at that early age. I still don't drink bellywash.

He lived in a beautiful two-story brick home, his name was Clark, and he was rich as six-foot-up-a-bull's-ass. He had a perfectly manicured lawn; but not long after we moved back to Bowling Green, he built a brick wall between our house and his. On his side, he had old brick, and on our side he put some cheap new brick. The wall was about eight feet tall and built purposely to keep us out of his yard; you couldn't see over it. But it didn't work; Brother could scale that wall with no trouble at all. We visited his yard frequently at night, fishing in his goldfish pool.

The Clarks had a son named O. V. He didn't run in the same circles that Brother and I ran in. We rarely saw him, and when we did see him, he was not overly friendly. Mother tells the tale from the time — when I was a first grader — that O. V. went home and told his mother he wanted to do something, and she said, "No, you can't do that." And he said, "Well, the Peyton boys do it." And his mother told him, "Well, you might as well get used to that. They're going to do a lot of things that you're not going to be allowed to do." And that was certainly true.

We didn't have much to do with people who had money. We were never members of the country club or anything like that. The Baptist Church told us the rich man had as much chance of getting into heaven as a camel going through the eye of a needle, which confirmed Brother's and my belief that they shouldn't be in heaven anyway. We suspected rich people didn't work, were probably fat, drank liquor, laid up in the morning, and probably stole the money they got, anyway. And that they just generally were trifling and no good—useless as tits on a boar hog. They damn sure didn't carry papers before daylight in the morning. The Baptists somehow conveyed the philosophy that it was better not to be "materialistic," and not to be rich—you'd do better. So Brother and I were very suspicious of rich people. We thought they were sissies. They didn't frequent our backyard or go to the river, so we never did see them much.

We went to the Baptist Church in Bowling Green. The Baptist preacher was named Reverend Skinner. He lived across and down the alley from us. Everybody in Bowling Green referred to him as "Reverend Skinner" or "Dr. Skinner," except Pa. Pa called him "Skinner." I remember one time I heard my great-aunt Cora asking Pa, "Please, don't call him 'Skinner'."

Pa didn't go to church if he could help it, and he usually could help it. I can remember going up there to the Baptist Church, the biggest and finest building in the county, and how they would hound us for money.

In Sunday School, they would say, "Last Sunday we had ninety-four people here and took in so much money; this Sunday we have ninety-six people and we want this much money." You wouldn't believe the pressure they'd put on you about money. They'd have three offerings: the regular offering, and extra offerings for the building fund and an offering for the starving Armenians. If one cause didn't get you, the next one would.

And they did know how to extract money. They knew Brother and I carried newspapers. It seemed they would focus on Brother because they knew Brother had money, and they wanted some of it. I go up there today and see that newer addition on the back, and I say my Brother and I helped when they were trying to build that some 40 years ago.

Shortly after we came back to Bowling Green, Mother decided the time had come for us to improve our social status. Although we hadn't got up to country club status yet, she decided the thing for us to do was join the Episcopal Church, which was down the street from our house about half a block. I remember that preacher's name was "Reverend Kershaw." One night when I was in the seventh grade, he came over to our house to visit and talk to the five of us about joining the Episcopal Church. He explained about communion and confirmation and there was a discussion about God.

Pa during that visit sat still and quiet and looked straight ahead and didn't open his mouth. Mother was doing the best she could, carrying most of the load of the conversation. Brother and I were sitting on the living room couch trying to keep a straight face. After that, Brother and I met Reverend Kershaw over at the church to talk about being baptized. On that occasion, he asked Brother what Mother and Father thought about the church and about religion. This terrified Mother when she found it out, and she questioned Brother, "Well, for goodness' sake, what did you tell him?"

Brother had told Reverend Kershaw that no one knew what Pa's religion was, 'cause he never mentioned it. And he had told Reverend Kershaw that he didn't know how Mother felt about the church, but she got up and did the very best she could do every day.

Pa had quit Spur Oil while we were in Nashville and had gone to work for People's Oil Company, a small independent company. After World War II, he left People's and went to work for Billups.

Billups bought Flashco, a small company headquartered in Jacksonville, Florida, with six service stations in Florida. Pa moved to Jacksonville in 1947 to run those stations. Mother and Sister went with him.

Brother and I stayed in Bowling Green and continued to live at 1220 State Street with my great-aunt, Cora Gaines, my mother's father's sister. She was very old, and must have been pushing eighty at that time. Cora had never married and was a devout Baptist. She was real delighted to have us there, did a great job for us and really did love us, as we loved her. I think it was fun for her, having the excitement of us and our friends in the house. She was a good sport, and I think she enjoyed the years we were up there.

When my parents and sister came to Jacksonville, they first rented an apartment. About a year after that, in 1948, they moved to Neptune Beach, where Pa had paid about $13,500 for a two-story shingle house at the northeast corner of First and South Streets.

Brother and I would come to Neptune Beach in the summer, but we stayed with Cora in Bowling Green during the school year. Because it was a college town and Western Kentucky University had no dormitories, Bowling Green had boarding houses filled with students. Brother and I ate breakfast and supper at a boarding house and had lunch at school.

Brother went to Bowling Green High School and I went from Bowling Green Junior High School to the high school, changing schools only once in the four years from seventh through the tenth grades.

Brother and I had complete freedom to do as we pleased. We had the run of the town. But Cora was a hard-shell Baptist. We ran pretty well loose most of the week, but Cora did most of the time make us go to church. The Baptist Church, the predominant social center of that county, was only one block away from us.

Cora was frugal and very, very religious, to put it mildly. She was against dancing, card playing, movies; in fact, she was against just about everything. And if anything came along that was not in a specific category, she said it was "materialistic," and that catchall would cover everything that you would like to do. I think as a result of that, I got kind of overdosed with religion.

Cora had no household help, and didn't want any. Extravagance of any kind was sinful. She even dressed in the closet by flashlight, on the premise that burning electric lights was extravagance. She was thin, had gray hair, and she was a very handsome woman.

During the years we lived in Bowling Green, Brother and I spent most of our weekends on the Barren River, which flowed about two miles from the center of town. We'd get there on our bikes. We could swim and fish down there, and camp out, and we also did some hunting. We had a rowboat and we knew every turn on the river in Warren County. That was the exciting place to be—on the river.

Pa used to call Bowling Green once in a while, checking on us. When he did, Cora's standard answer was, "Oh, they're not here, they're down by the river." Brother and I had some great times.

We were very interested in the sports teams and athletics, and we both had paper routes. We got up at four-thirty in the morning to carry the Louisville morning paper, the Courier-Journal. At times, we carried the Park City Daily News, the Bowling Green paper, in the afternoon. We didn't carry the papers in both the morning and the afternoon, but we always had one paper route or the other.

We carried the papers on bikes, which was fine until we had snow. Then we couldn't ride the bikes and had to trudge through the snow for five miles, starting before daylight every morning. Sometimes I wouldn't get to school until nine or nine-thirty. It was a tough way to make a few dollars. We'd be totally exhausted, and did not do so hot in school on the days it snowed.

We were responsible for delivering the papers and collecting the money, and got a commission on what we collected. We were making six dollars a week, sometimes eight, which back then was a lot of money, and more than any of the other boys in our neighborhood had.

In addition to our paper route, Brother and I had the neighborhood job of carrying out all the slop. It really was slop, because in those days there were no garbage disposals. There were three houses in a row, all duplexes: ours and our cousin Underwood Hines' and one next to his, each with apartments upstairs and down. Brother and I, for a dollar a week from each group, would haul the slop cans each day from the back porches out to the alley where we emptied them into drums for pickup, then hauled the cans back to the porches. The wood steps from the upstairs apartments were rather steep, and on snowy and icy days, they were treacherous. I remember having bad falls.

Brother would carry slop one day and I'd carry the next day. We'd been doing this for some time, when I discovered that if I skipped a day, Brother would never know it. He'd just have a big load the next day. Well, Brother figured this out about the same time, so we both wound up skipping, and we had much unhappiness in the neighborhood, about the slop.

We also had the job of stoking a furnace in the wintertime. In our house, we had gas heaters. Underwood's house also had natural gas, but the third house had a coal furnace, and we went over there every afternoon after school and took the clinkers out and put the coal in and stoked it for the night. As a result of our activities, Brother and I always had a little money on us.

In our backyard, we had a basketball goal, and a horseshoe court with real horseshoes. There were always ten or twelve boys there, and nearly always a basketball game going on, most any time after school and all weekend. We played basketball year 'round, except in the dead of winter. Then we'd go slip into the gym at Bowling Green High School or Western Kentucky University.

Most of the things in that town were within walking distance, or certainly biking range, because the downtown square was just three blocks away. We could walk to the movie down there, and Western Kentucky was about three blocks in the other direction, and the high school was about four blocks.

Each city block had an alley down the middle, dividing the back yards. Alleys were Brother's and my main arteries of travel, and we usually used them instead of the main streets. We knew the contents of everybody's back yards for blocks around. On occasion, when we needed some particular item, we would know which back yard it would be in, and we would salvage it come nightfall.

If all roads led to Rome, surely all alleys led to the Peyton boys' house. Our centrally located house was kind of a center of social activity for our friends, since Brother and I lived as if we were at summer camp all the time, completely unsupervised. Because Cora was upstairs praying.

She might have prayed even more fervently if she had realized how much poker was being played right in our back yard. At night, there was much screaming and hollering about the bets. Brother and I usually prevailed in the poker game because we were well financed by the revenues from our paper routes. We could buy and bluff our way through, usually. The circle of crouched boys intent on penny-nickel-quarter ante gambling in our Army surplus pup tent would have seemed a den of iniquity to Cora, but the "poker face" I developed while sizing up the competition those long summer nights was to be an invaluable blessing in business dealings many years later.

In reality, 1220 State Street was the free zone of Bowling Green, where all boys could come at any time, and while they were at 1220 they were completely free of any supervision, restrictions, or adult standards of behavior.

Despite our lack of supervision, we and our friends escaped permanent disabilities. I do remember one time, we had a basketball game going on, and a horseshoe pitching game at the same time, and the basketball got away and came over the backboard, and Jim Kimbrough came running after it at the same time Brother was releasing a horseshoe. The shoe hit Kimbrough up beside the head and blood rained down, and Kimbrough didn't say a word. He turned white as a sheet and started running home down the alley behind the house. Brother was right after him, telling him, "Come on back, Kimbrough, you'll be alright."

He didn't come back. We didn't see Kimbrough for about a week, but he got alright.

Brother was kind of the ringleader of the neighborhood. He was an authority on fishing, hunting, and knew all the turns of the river and where the fish were. And Brother didn't suffer from inactivity. He was either playing sports or fishing, full time. Brother had a way of living in his own world, having his own interests, and they didn't require a lot of friends. He would be glad to take people with him on his fishing or grappling trips, or running his trap lines, but it wasn't necessary. He was very quiet and calm, and everybody liked him.

Another attraction at our house was the goldfish pond next door, behind the two-story frame boarding house owned by our cousin Underwood. Brother would catch fish in the river or lakes and if the fish were of any size, or there was anything significant about the fish, we'd haul them back alive in lard cans and put them in the fish pond. We always had a collection of bass, brim, and catfish. It was a great source of entertainment throughout that end of town, to come by and see what fish were in the pool.

I can remember carrying fish home through the woods in a five-gallon lard can full of water. In Kentucky language for exhaustion, I had strained milk, but Brother was saying, "We've got to hurry and get him to the pool. He's turning bottom up!" And I'd take a few more steps before buckling under the weight of the lard can.

Back in those days in Kentucky we had no car at all. Our mode of transportation was bicycle or walk. In fact, there were months and months when I never got in a car. There was no television. And the biggest source of entertainment in the town were sports and fishing.

Bowling Green was a very sports-oriented town. And we played all the rival towns around there, every year on the same schedule, at the same time. They would play in Bowling Green one year and in the opposing town the next. It was kind of one town against the other one, and they had great spirit. Sports activities were really the core of the whole social center of Bowling Green.

The rivalries were unbelievable. School spirit and the dedication of the entire community was focused on beating Glasgow, and Owensboro, and Scottsboro, and Hopkinsville, and Russellville; and much of the county would turn out for the games. There'd be a pep rally at school in the morning, and we actually waged a small war against those towns; our major rivals were "Hoptown" and Owensboro. Every game was kind of what a mini-Georgia-Florida game would be down here in north

Florida. Brother played high school football and I played junior high football and basketball.

Elvis Donaldson was coach at Bowling Green High School, and he made a tremendous impression on me. I guess he was really my role model during those important years. I lived away from my parents for five years during junior high and high school.

Coach Donaldson was about thirty years old at that time. We all thought he was John Wayne and Sergeant York and Audie Murphy all rolled into one. In addition to coaching football and basketball, Coach Donaldson was a teacher. He had played football for Western Kentucky University, and he was about five-foot-ten and very tough

When he gave a pep talk before the game, I'd remember every word, and still do to this day. He was referred to simply as "Coach," as he still is. And when he told us to do something, we tried like hell to do it. Coach Donaldson had what we call in the military "command presence." When he walked into the room, the room suddenly became quiet and seemed smaller. He had our absolute and complete attention.

I never heard him raise his voice, but he could give you a stern look that was more severe than any words. He demanded a lot of respect, and got it. Coach was the greatest leader and motivator I have ever been around.

Coach told us not to eat peanuts because it would cut our wind. I never did understand what medical authority he based that on, but even today I do not eat peanuts because it cuts your wind.

Brother played end on the varsity team. The Bowling Green newspaper best described Brother's football ability. They said he was small, but "tough as shoe leather on defense." I remember in his senior year the first game was with Hopkinsville, which back in that day was the local power in that end of Kentucky. Hopkinsville had great teams and always seemed to beat us.

I can remember Coach Donaldson told us after practice the afternoon before the game, that he had waited years to have a team with the ability we had, that we had the talent in every position, and this was our year—we were going to surprise Hopkinsville the next day.

The game was played at Western Kentucky's football stadium on top of the hill. Hopkinsville got ahead 19 to 6 in the first half. At half-time, Coach was very calm, said everything was going to be alright, we were right where we needed to be, that we were in better shape than they were, they would tire and we wouldn't, in the last quarter. We believed him.

Of course, everybody on the team played two-way football, both offense and defense, which meant the players were on the field for the whole game. Therefore football was not only a game of hard knocks, but required a lot of stamina.

Coach told the team never to sit or lie down during timeouts. We could go down on one knee. The other team would be over there gasping for breath and lying down flat on their backs, and he wouldn't let us show any signs of fatigue. Coach said, "Never let them know how tired you are; if they knew they'd come after you." This was a lesson I have remembered all my life. I have never conveyed to anybody any fear, and in business I have never let anybody know how bad we were hurting financially at times.

In the hot September afternoon, sure enough, the

Hopkinsville players, who were bigger and heavier, got tired. The game wound up tied at 25 to 25, one of the best high school football games the long suffering Bowling Green fans have ever seen, Brother played the entire game, got in a few key tackles, and there was much excitement in Bowling Green.

The other big rivalry, besides "Hoptown," was Owensboro. During Brother's junior year, we went to Owensboro for a night game on a lighted field. Owensboro had a great team that year, and I remember they ran out on the field dressed in black uniforms. Everything was black except their white socks, shoelaces, and the numbers on their uniforms. Their black helmets were so shiny that the field lights reflected in them. Owensboro ran out in perfect formation and went through their calisthenics, and they looked like Nazis. I have never been so terrified in my life.

They had an all-state end named Gipe. He was six-foot-four and weighed 220 pounds. Back in those days, that was big. Coach asked Brother the day before the game if he could handle Gipe. Brother assured him that he could.

The first time Bowling Green had the ball on their own 30-yard line, Brother lined up across from Gipe. All eyes were on Gipe, and I can remember the play was to come around Gipe's end. Gipe advanced over the line of scrimmage and picked Brother up by the seat of the pants and the nape of the neck and threw him at the ball carrier. When the confused referee blew his whistle, Brother and half the Bowling Green backfield were sprawled out on the ground and Gipe was standing amongst them. The whole crowd was hushed, because they knew it was going to be a long game, and it was. Owensboro beat the hell out of us. They had us 21 to 0 at the half, and it was downhill from then on.

The next year was the year we tied "Hoptown," and this time Owensboro came to Bowling Green and again they dressed in black and again they beat us, but it was a close game, 19 to 12. It was a good show and Coach was proud of us.

About this time, I had visions of being an all-state football player. In fact, that was my real desire, to be at least a good running back at Bowling Green High School. Brother and I were very health conscious. I remember, back in those days, of course you knew nothing about dope or anything like that. Some of the boys in high school smoked, but they told me smoking stunts your growth and I was already little and skinny, so that was enough of a deterrent for me; I never touched a cigarette. I never drank anything with alcohol until I got out of the Army when I was twenty-two years old. We did work very hard at athletics.

All the time my athletic ability was mediocre at best, but I thought I was a lot better than I was being given credit for, and I thought the coach failed to recognize how good I was. It wasn't until years later when I looked back that I realized that I really didn't have much going for me. I had two undesirable attributes: littleness and slowness. I didn't have any one really outstanding ability, other than being in great shape. I did have more endurance than any of the other boys on the basketball and football teams, because of rowing the river, and riding the Schwinn bike with the paper route.

I played football and basketball at Bowling Green, and later, at Fletcher High in Neptune Beach, Florida, and in Evergreen, Colorado. I did fair.

I loved the game and loved being on the team, more than probably anybody else did. Being part of the team and the spirit was just the biggest thing in my life at that time, and I can remember every boy that started for the Bowling Green football team during those years, in every position, and can recall most of the games—what happened during the games and what the final score was.

We did have some good football players in Bowling Green. There was a boy named Bobby Bilyeu in my seventh grade class. We all thought that someday Bobby would be an all-state halfback for Bowling Green High School. That was about as good as anyone could do.

This boy was small and grew to be about 5'6", but he was extremely fast and he had the ability to accelerate instantly. You could reach out to grab him and he would just change gears and almost leap away from you. He also had the ability to change directions running at full speed. He was the most natural runner I have ever seen. He did make all-state at Bowling Green High School during his senior year, in the fall of 1949. He was a great athlete.

Bowling Green had great basketball teams back in that period. We had several All-State basketball players. There were district basketball tournaments and regionals and then you went to the state tournament in Louisville. Schools were not matched by size, they just played—every school in the state.

We had Bobo Davenport, an All-State guard, and he played against Ralph Beard, who was later an All-American at Kentucky.

Back in those days, one of the main weapons in basketball was a two-handed set shot from out beyond the foul circle. The teams would come down and the guard would shoot a two-handed set shot. A good guard, when he was having a hot night, would arch the ball through the center of the hoop to swish against the bottom of the net. It was quite an athletic feat.

Bobo Davenport was a champion at this and he was so cocky that he would come down, set up a two-handed set shot, shoot a high arching ball, and before it hit the bottom of the net he would turn around and start running down the court like he knew it was going to hit. The gym would go wild.

During wintertime in Kentucky, we would resort to taking the basketball to a gym on Saturday morning. Slipping into a locked gym was quite a feat. Brother could get into any gym in the county, given adequate time.

The best gym in the county was Western Kentucky University's. They had great teams back in that day, and had national ranking and a beautiful gymnasium. The floors were polished to absolute perfection.

This magnificent concrete structure was on top of the hill and had two levels of cellars. The locker rooms were underneath the gymnasium, and below the locker rooms was the heating cellar. On Saturdays, the gym doors were locked and in addition they were secured with log chains on the inside.

I can remember many cold Saturdays, we'd slip over to the gym with a rope. Each window in the lowest level was at the bottom of a window well that held the earth away from the foundation to allow light and air to reach the cellar window. At the top of this shaft, a waist-high rail prevented passersby from falling in. Brother tied our rope to the rail and we let ourselves down the rope to the window, which wasn't locked because nobody thought anyone could get down there.

We would then come up through the two cellars with our basketball. We would take about two boys with us, and would be up there having a nice game on Saturday morning, in that immaculate gymnasium, running back and forth. Coach Ed Diddle, Western's famous basketball coach, walking through the gym, would come up there and scream at the top of his voice, "Get off our floor!"

We'd come over to him and, before he threw us out of the gym, he would always say, "How did you get in here?" And we'd point to the door which had log chains on it and was locked. And he'd bring out more chains. He never did know how we got in there, and it happened several times every winter.

The hill on which the gymnasium stood also provided momentum for Soapbox Derby cars. When I was fourteen years old, in the summer between my eighth and ninth grade, I entered the Soapbox Derby and won. It was quite an event; I think there were twenty-six racers. Brother and I built the racer out of aluminum. It was sponsored by a restaurant called the University Inn.

The whole town gathered at the hillside and we raced two at a time all afternoon, and I won six heats. Bowling Green's Park City News ran the headline, "6,000 Watch Peyton Win the Soapbox Derby." Brother was very proud, and I went to the nationals in Akron, Ohio.

Over a hundred racers were in Akron from all over the country. I was picked by the Associated Press as one of three to win, on the theory that the racer and I weighed a total of 250 pounds, which was the maximum weight allowed. And I sat right over the back axle with most of my weight on that one axle, which the experts said was much to be desired—an excellent way for the weight to be distributed.

The track up there was beautiful and there were a lot of spectators, and it was the big time. On the first heat, the other racers ran off and left me. They had balanced their wheels, which I knew nothing about, and I was out of my league. Anyway, it was a lot of fun, and very exciting.

In Bowling Green, because of school, carrying papers, sports, fishing, camping, poker playing, and so forth, Brother and I never suffered from inactivity. We were always on the move.

A Bowling Green neighbor who was in the used tire business must have had a thousand tires in his back yard. He had some tractor tires higher than our heads. Brother and I would go down there by way of the alley on occasion and get a tire or two. Late one night, Brother and I took two of his tractor tires, rolled them down the alley, into the street, and about three blocks up a real steep hill.

From the hilltop, we could sight straight down to the foot of the hill, where the street deadended into a cross street. On the far side of this cross street, dimly visible in the dark, was a white brick house, like a target at the end of a rifle range.

Brother and I hid these tires in the bushes at the top of the hill, and then when the coast was clear, rolled a tire out into the middle of the street and gave it a good shove. It picked up speed to a good thirty or thirty-five miles an hour on the downhill run, going down the street wide open. The tire crossed the cross-street, hit the curb on the far side, jumped up in the air about ten feet and hit the house broadside, shaking it to its foundations.

It didn't hit the windows, it hit the wall. But it sounded

like thunder when it hit. The lights came on in the house, the people went out and saw the tire and there was much discussion, then they went back in. Brother and I were watching from the bushes at the top of the hill. When they went back in and turned off the lights, we let the second missile loose.

I remember Brother was running alongside the tire, making sure it would roll straight, and we got it rolling right down the center of the street, until it got going so fast that he couldn't keep up with it, and then we'd run back and hide in the bushes.

The second tire hit the curb, bounced up in the air about ten feet, and broadsided the house. The lights came on again, and this time we heard police sirens. Brother and I ran down the alley, laughing all the way.

Another thing we used to do, in the winter, was throw snowballs at cars. The game was to get drivers to stop, get out, and chase you, and then see if you could outrun them. We knew all the turns and secret places in the alleys, and the person chasing us was running in a strange area on snow and ice and didn't have a chance to catch us. One night, Brother and I were throwing snowballs at cars from a cross street, and a car stopped. The driver started chasing us.

Brother ran down a narrow walkway between the Baptist Church and the Sunday School building. It was black as Egypt in there at night, and this walkway had a dogleg to the left. Brother had forgotten that, and was running wide open when he hit that wall. It almost knocked him out. I was right behind him, but I stopped in time. Brother was on the ground moaning, and I was afraid the man was going to catch us, but he didn't want to come down that dark passage that far. I tried to keep Brother quiet until the man went on back and got in his car; then I pissanted Brother home over my shoulder. His knee hurt him for a couple of months.

My four years in Bowling Green were the good years. I changed schools from Bowling Green Junior High to Bowling Green Senior High, and that was the only school I stayed in long enough to not be Newboy. I really did fit in, we had good times, good friends, and we were unique because we had no supervision. Some of the families up there were reluctant at that time to let their youngsters go with the Peyton boys because they knew we were completely unsupervised and did things they didn't approve of.

But when Brother and I announced our plan to build a boat and float down the four rivers linking Bowling Green to New Orleans, nobody believed even the Peyton boys would really try that.

—Chapter Three—

The River Rat

As you know, Brother and I spent most of our youth on the rivers and creeks of Tennessee and Kentucky. Even back in my grammar school days, I was vaguely aware that all of these rivers and creeks wound up as part of the Mississippi River. When we moved back to Bowling Green, occasionally tugboats would push barges up from the Ohio and Green rivers to the Barren River at Bowling Green and dock at the old boat landing. Brother and I had many visits and conversations with the deck hands on these pushboats.

They told us tales of the Mississippi River. They told us how the Mississippi River swallowed all the rivers and in its treacherous waters lurked many dangers. There were whirlpools that would suck a small boat under, and sometimes logs bigger than telephone poles would float down the river and sink small boats. They told us about big eddies, which would force boats upstream. And they told us that the rats that hung out on the wharves were as big as cats and would come right on your boat when you were docked and attack you.

They described in detail the big paddle wheel boats that ran up and down the Mississippi, pushing as many as twelve to sixteen barges, and said they would make no effort to go around you if you got in front of them; they would blow their horn to warn you and then run right over the top of you. They warned us that these boats ran twenty-four hours a day, and at night or in a heavy fog or rainstorm it was impossible for them to see you and they made no effort to maneuver around you. They said that on the river bank there were many river pirates who were really vagrant thugs, existing by robbing and stealing whatever was on the river.

Brother would listen to these tales again and again, and although he never said, I knew exactly what he was planning. In the dead of winter in 1947-1948, when I was a sophomore at Bowling Green High School and Brother was a freshman at Western Kentucky, we decided the time had come to challenge the mighty Mississippi. I was 16, five-foot-six and weighed 125 pounds. Brother was five-foot-ten and weighed 150 pounds.

As the weeks and months went by, we developed our plan to build a boat in the back yard, a small kind of flatbottom rowboat with a cabin on it. Our plan was to put it in the river at Bowling Green and float down to New Orleans, by way of the Barren River to the Green River, Green River to the Ohio, Ohio to the Mississippi. This route was 1,363 miles. At first, nobody thought we were serious about going to New Orleans, but as the boat took shape in the early spring of 1948, people realized we were dead serious.

Brother and I decided we needed more than just the two of us, we wanted a crew of four. Getting the other two was not easy to do, because the parents of our friends would not even consider letting their boys go over thirteen hundred miles on a flatbottom boat to New Orleans.

Volunteers were not forthcoming.

We invited Hugh David Roe, who was later the only boy I know of that was captain of the football, basketball and baseball teams at Bowling Green High School; Bob Dickey, who later attended Vanderbilt Law School and is practicing law in Louisville now; and Jay Bettersworth. These boys were our closest friends, and they expressed a desire to go, but their parents would not even discuss allowing them go on such a trip. We did finally get another couple of boys. James Chestnut and Bobby Faxon agreed to go, and the four of us set out down the Barren River in the best tradition of Mark Twain.

About two weeks before we started down, Pa called up and asked us when we'd be home, and we told him we were coming home by the river instead of coming on the bus. Coming to New Orleans. Pa didn't pay much attention to this at first because he didn't believe it. Later, he didn't like it much, but he didn't particularly care one way or the other.

The amazing thing, looking back at it, is that during that trip our folks didn't know where in the hell we were. They'd never seen the boat or anything. And they didn't seem overly concerned. They wanted to know how long it would take to get down there, and we said, "Maybe a month," and they said, "Well, hope you have a good trip. Let us know when you get to New Orleans."

Back that spring, we just took hammer and nails and got started. We built the boat out of used lumber, and two layers of tongue and groove 1 x 6s for the bottom, and the gunwales were built out of 2 x 12s. The cabin walls were plywood with battens at the joints. Understand that Cora didn't have any materials to build the boat, but by way of Bowling Green's alleys, we had access to everybody's back yard.

I've told about the man with tires in his back yard. Another man had stacked in his back yard many thousands of board feet of different sizes of lumber; therein lay our source of lumber. Another neighbor had the tarpaper we used for roofing. Another neighbor had some used windows.

We didn't go up there and get the lumber all in one night. The theory was that if we took a little bit every night or so, he wouldn't miss it. All during the winter, we'd get up at night and go up to his back yard and take a few boards at a time, so he wouldn't miss them. Over a period of months, we stockpiled the lumber and other materials in the attic of the old frame storeroom out in back of our garage, near the alley.

Brother would hand each piece up to me, and I remember one night I had a 1 x 6 halfway into the attic, at arm's length. There was no light—we were being very secretive—and suddenly we heard hounds baying. We thought they'd turned the bloodhounds loose on us. Brother told me to freeze; the hounds were coming down the alley. I held the 1 x 6 in midair until my arms trembled. We were sure that the hounds were coming after us, but they ran right on down the alley and passed by us. We had enough wood, come spring, to build the boat.

It was a rectangle eighteen feet long, eight feet wide, and the bow was built like a barge; in other words, it didn't have a point on it, it had a slanted bow. And then it had a cabin which housed four bunks, a double-decker on each side, with chicken wire for the springs, and we had sleeping bags. It was really quite comfortable.

There was no toilet. We had pressurized propane Coleman lanterns and a propane gas Coleman stove for the kitchen. We painted the boat dark brown with some kind of old navy or army paint, and on the side in black letters we wrote "River Rat." Brother nailed a coon hide on the cabin door. We had rails made from galvanized pipe and cleats made from wood.

After we built this boat, which took several months, we got a mover to come with a flat-bed truck. He used jacks to load the boat onto the truck, and hauled it from our back yard to the river for us. And we launched the River Rat in the Barren River.

That night, the damn thing almost sank. We had so much trouble with it leaking, we had to stay up all night bailing 'til the wood swelled and the leaks slowed down. We had put tar on the bottom when we built it, and we caulked it after we got it in the water. It leaked a little bit from then on, but it didn't leak much. It was a pretty riverworthy boat.

We set out Saturday morning, June 4, 1948, the day after school let out. Several people gathered at the boat dock to see us off. It was indeed a proud and happy day. The first part of the trip, on the Barren and the Green Rivers, was very pleasant and we made good progress. These rivers were small and the tree canopy almost covered them, so we were in the shade a good deal of the time. The water was green and flowed at a gentle but steady pace through the lush green hills of Kentucky. We had deck chairs on the front deck, a portable radio, and we were in high spirits.

Along the way we would pass fishermen and people sitting on their docks. They were always very friendly and curious as to where we were going. When we told them we were going to New Orleans, they didn't believe us, so after awhile we just quit telling people that.

When we approached the locks on the Barren and the Green Rivers, we had some close calls, coming around the bend and having to get away from the dam, over to the lock side of the river. If you were to get caught on the dam, and get pulled over the dam, of course that would be bad. We had to row very hard sometimes, to keep from getting washed over the dam and to get into the slot for the lock. But we always made it.

The pace and excitement picked up the day the Green River dumped into the Ohio River. Several days later, when we hit Cairo, Illinois, where the Ohio flows into the Mississippi, we all had a funny feeling that the good times were over.

When we rounded the bend and saw the Mississippi for the first time, we were all in awe. The Mississippi was not only unbelievably big, it was muddy and swift. You see, Old Man River had come down all the way from Minnesota and was half mad by the time he got to Cairo and was anxious to get to New Orleans.

And when the Ohio started butting into the waters of the Mississippi, you could see where the two waters joined, because the Mississippi was muddy brown and the Ohio was green. Old Man River didn't flow, he rolled. And as he rolled into the Ohio, he made strange gurgling, lapping, swallowing noises.

People we had talked to on the Ohio River had told us the River Rat would never survive the Mississippi. Again, we heard terrible tales about the big boats, whirlpools, driftwood and the eddies. So by the time we hit the Mississippi, we were very apprehensive, to put it mildly.

We were concerned whether the River Rat would hold up under such severe turbulence. Our first day on the Mississippi, a big paddle wheeler came up and nearly swamped us, and we knew we were in the big leagues, and had tough days ahead.

And we did have tough days. Late in the afternoon, we would start trying to find a sandbar we could pull up on to be out of the waves, away from the rocking, and away from the woods, swamps and levees so there were no insects. The big boats ran twenty-four hours a day, but they could not hit us on the sandbar and we would be safe while we were asleep.

The boat, being squared-off and without a keel, couldn't handle a head wind, and we would just pull up on a sandbar and stay there for awhile. Sometimes we couldn't get to a sandbar, and would pull up to the bank. The Rat was not aerodynamic, so the wind was our biggest enemy, and I think that is why even today I don't like wind. Even when we did not have a head wind, if we had a wind from the east or west, we had a constant struggle to keep from being blown where we didn't want to be.

Rainstorms and fog were also our bitter enemies, because in those conditions we couldn't see well enough to stay close to the banks and out of the channel. The River Rat's grayish brown color meant the big boats couldn't see us. And they damn sure would have run over us. We would have been better off if the Rat had been white or some other light color. The big boats couldn't stay out of our way; we had to stay out of their way. So in bad weather we usually wound up on a sandbar, waiting for better conditions.

Each of the four rivers was swifter than the last. As we got down the Mississippi, its current got even stronger, and we were able to make five or six miles an hour, pretty steadily. Where the riverbanks narrowed the channel, it could be swifter than that. With the current plus a tailwind, we could really move out and probably hit ten miles per hour. As we got going down the Mississippi River, we got better and better at playing the currents and reading the charts, and we could make fifty miles on a good day and some days with a tailwind, we made even more. The whole trip took a month.

We devised different methods of steering the boat. We had a little rowboat hooked onto the stern of the River Rat, just like a tugboat, with bumpers on it. We'd get back there and row the rowboat, and push the River Rat. We also found out the easiest way to steer the Rat was to have an oar off the front deck. We could swing the bow around easier from the front than from the back. We took fifteen-minute shifts of rowing and steering, and then thirty minutes off. We'd rest in the cabin until it was our turn again. We were exhausted all the time, not only from the physical exertion but also from constant apprehension about boats running over us.

The River Rat became weary from the strain and turbulence of the Mississippi, and it began to leak more and more. Therefore, we had to take turns bailing as well as rowing on the latter part of the trip. By the time we hit New Orleans, we were spending just about as much time bailing as we were rowing.

We had bought river charts from the Corps of Engineers in Bowling Green, and we tried to look ahead to keep from running aground and keep away from the deep channels used by big boats. Most of the time we knew where we were, because with those charts you look at the landmarks; you don't need a compass. The Rat probably drew about ten inches of water, so we could go in extremely shallow water. If we ran aground, which we did sometimes, we would just get off into the water and push the Rat off; it was manageable.

From talking to the river people, we knew the names of some of the biggest boats on the river and we watched for them. The River Rat could not handle the wakes of those big boats; the wave would come up a couple of feet high, washing over our deck, and we'd close the doors to keep the water out of the cabin as best we could and then bail.

Early one morning the biggest boat we'd ever seen was coming up the river. We all got ready and moved over closer to shore and tried to batten down everything. The name of that boat was the Harry S. Truman, and it was pushing twelve barges. The waves it put off were at least six feet tall. And The Rat came very close to sinking. But we managed to bail it and get it going again. What made it so tough that time was that we were in a narrow channel; we couldn't get away from the danger. Usually the river was wide enough for us to get far enough away from those big boats so they wouldn't sink us.

The other big boat that we watched for was the Sprague. Sure enough, one morning we saw it bearing down on us, but the river was wide enough that we could get away from it, so it didn't hurt us too bad.

Another trouble we had on the Mississippi River was that a couple of times the river rose, and all kinds of driftwood and even trees four and five feet in diameter were coming down the river. We had to be very careful about logs running into The Rat in swift water. A tree trunk striking the side of the River Rat would have sunk us. And sometimes we'd be going along close to the shore and we'd get into these eddies, a kind of circular motion, and we'd wind up going upstream temporarily. We learned how to play those eddies, though.

One of our biggest fears on the Mississippi was the whirlpools, which were usually near the eddies and sometimes were big enough to start spinning The Rat round and round. They were terrifying because of the gurgling noise they made. We learned how to row out of them by keeping the bow straight with the oar off the front and rowing hard from the rowboat in the back, but those whirlpools scared our mule.

We had a lot of trouble with eating on the boat. When we got to New Orleans, I had lost ten pounds, because the diet on The Rat was not so hot. We didn't have any refrigeration. Everybody kicked in a little bit to buy groceries, but we didn't really buy enough. We carried about a hundred pounds of potatoes; most of the time we made french fries. And we also carried a lot of canned goods: pork and beans, applesauce and others. We did fix toast and jelly. We didn't have anything to drink except water. We kept iodine on board, and when we ran out of water, we sterilized the river water with the iodine. We had to be awfully thirsty to drink it.

We stopped at towns along the way and would go in and get a good meal, fill our water jugs, and get a few groceries, like eggs and bread. Then we'd stop occasionally out on the riverbank and scout the land and nearby farms, and forage for whatever was available. Which wasn't much in June, because that early in the year, most of the crops weren't ready. We always spent the night on the boat.

And we did do some fishing coming down the river. We caught some fish, but not many, because we were always on the move, the water was usually muddy and swift, and we had to keep rowing to keep the boat going. Our attire was usually shorts and tee shirts, which were usually dirty with a brown river grime.

We had a lot of trouble on that boat. The stress affected us all in different ways. We were never particularly relaxed because there was always the unknown in front of us. We were in such close quarters that with the tension we became very irritable and suspicious of each other.

Brother became kind of the captain of the boat, and kind of directed everything, and he and I continued to get along in spite of the tension. But when something was missing, there was always the feeling that one of the other two boys got it. I remember one day we were trying to fix something and couldn't find the hammer, and Brother said, "Faxon stole that hammer." And he really thought that at the time. But of course, how could he steal it on the boat? What he would do with it, or why he would want to steal it I don't know, but we were awfully young to be under that prolonged period of stress.

At night, we'd put up in shallow water on a sandbar where there weren't any mosquitoes. Although we had anchors and lines, there was always fear that while we were sleeping the River Rat might break loose from our anchor and float down the river. The waves from passing boats were kind of nerve-wracking because we always imagined that we were floating down the river and about to be run over.

One of the boys with us, James Chestnut, couldn't finish the trip. He started having bad dreams, and became delirious, and he'd wake up in the middle of the night and run through the cabin hollering, "We're about to get hit! A boat's coming over us!" He was imagining that The Rat was loose and was about to get hit by a big boat, and he got worse and worse. He got where he didn't get any sleep. Finally, he just gave out and we put him ashore at Helena, Arkansas, and he caught a bus home.

When you're coming down the Mississippi, you don't see much in the way of surrounding countryside, because of the levees on each side of the river. All we could see was the bank, with some trees and foliage. We seldom saw a farmhouse or anything, except when we got to a town on a bluff, like Memphis or Helena, or Vicksburg.

The river turns so much that you sometimes think you're not making much progress. There's a story about this fellow coming down the Mississippi in a rowboat. He stopped one night and spent the night at this house, and he got up and rowed all day and that night he pulled in to spend the night at another farmhouse, and when he realized it was the same farmhouse he'd left that morning, the frustration drove him crazy as a bat.

We had hit the Mississippi where the Ohio and Mississippi join at Cairo, Illinois. As we came on down, newspaper reporters first met us in Memphis. And then we saw them in Helena, Arkansas; and Vicksburg, Mississippi; and Baton Rouge, and in every little town as we came downriver. And they'd take pictures and interview us. As we went along, the reporters made sure that a lot of people knew where we were on the river.

We and the River Rat were going to be featured in a Paramount newsreel, but we got to New Orleans sooner than we had expected. It was the July Fourth holiday weekend and the Paramount people weren't there yet. But we were met on the dock by the mayor of New Orleans and several newspaper reporters.

We had called Pa in Florida when we had stopped in Baton Rouge. He told us that he would be in New Orleans on business and for us to check into the Jung Hotel and that he would see us there.

Once we got to the hotel and checked in, we all took long hot showers, the first we'd had in over a month. And, sure enough that afternoon, Pa knocked on the door. It was a good thing he showed up because we were near broke.

Pa didn't give a damn about the newsreel, and wouldn't let us wait for Paramount. But the Associated Press reported the trip and we were in newspapers all over the country. They called us the "modern day Huckleberry Finn and Tom Sawyer. "

Hell, our story was even in Canadian newspapers. Wayne Levitt, who is now President of Gate Marketing, remembers it being in his paper in Arkansas when he was a boy.

We left The River Rat in New Orleans on the side of the river. We tried to sell it but there were no buyers, so we gave it to a black man who was down there fishing. I've often wondered what happened to The Rat.

In Jacksonville, the newspaper said we were from Neptune Beach. The fact was that Mother and Pa lived in Neptune Beach, but Brother and I had never lived there and of course nobody knew us.

About thirty years after our trip on the River Rat, I went back to Bowling Green when we were building a Gate service station up there. I was driving over the bridge at the Barren River with this real estate man, and he didn't know who the hell I was. I said, "Is that the Barren River?" And he said, "Yeah." I said, "Where does that river go?" He said, "Hell, it goes all the way down to the Mississippi River. You can go down that river all the way to New Orleans." And I said, "Is that right?" He said, "Yeah, as a matter of fact, we had some boys that did that one time about thirty years ago; got in right here and went all the way to New Orleans!" I didn't respond.

As far as I know, we're the only ones who ever made

that journey. In retrospect, I think managing the logistics of that trip at our age was quite a feat, and the most amazing thing about it was that Pa would tolerate such an expedition. But Pa only thought about his own self.

—Chapter Four—

Florida

When we moved to Florida in 1948, we moved to South Street in Neptune Beach. I came down out of the lush green hills of Kentucky, where I had been very active and very much at home. Up there, we never had an idle moment. We got up at 4:30 in the morning and were busy into the night. Our house at 1220 State Street was the center of activity for all the neighborhood. The years in Kentucky had been free and fun.

Moving to Florida was for me like moving to the Sahara Desert. Neptune Beach didn't have one full-grown tree. There was no foliage except those scrawny palm trees that looked like the puffs on a poodle's tail, and there was no dirt, just sand, and it was flat and bare. No leafy woods, no hills, no creeks. I didn't feel at home there. It was very hard for me to adjust to the beach, and in fact, Brother never adjusted to the beach. He brought his traps with him, but there was no place to put them; there were no creeks for grappling; and the beach didn't do much for Brother. That was the only place that Brother moved where he just didn't seem to fit.

Brother and I needed money as usual. We had one of those little push mowers, and we put an ad in the paper: "We cut grass, 60¢ an hour," and a phone number. Pa's advice was, "Put in there, 'We do anything for 60¢ an hour.'" Brother said no, there were some things he wouldn't do for sixty cents an hour. Brother never did stay down here too long. He kept going back to Western Kentucky to school.

Now I had hit town like a stray dog in a new neighborhood; I was slipping around and walking on tiptoes. I knew absolutely no one. My first association with Fletcher High School was when I went out for football in August, just two weeks before school started. I had much trouble running, because I couldn't get traction in the sand. I had trouble with the Florida heat. I was not exactly welcomed by the team—in fact, I was ignored.

When classes started at Fletcher High School I was a junior, 16 years old, and my fellow students were not overly friendly. I sat on the back row and once again they called me Newboy.

I went out for football and tried my best, but didn't get noticed. I practiced all week but then came game time. I was available, I sat on the bench, but I didn't get to play in the games.

Brother was still up at Western Kentucky, going to school. Cora died, and Brother rented a room in one of the neighbor's houses. This was the first time Brother and I had ever been separated in all of our upbringing and it was a tough time. I remember that period as lonely.

I had my tonsils out at St. Luke's Hospital in late September of 1948. Dr. Marshall Taylor did the surgery and I was supposed to get well quick, but I didn't. I had a lot of trouble, and it knocked hell out of me. I must have been out of school for about two weeks.

When I got well, I had this peculiar whistle. I could whistle without moving my lips. And I could whistle both inhaling and exhaling air, and at first I wasn't even aware of that.

The first time I whistled in school, I was amazed, because the teacher was so confused. I didn't move my lips, and it was kind of a ringing noise. I was sitting there and my mouth was just barely open. I remember how startled the teacher was, and how mad she got, because she didn't know what the noise was, or where it was coming from. She didn't think it was me. I found that I could use that whistle as a weapon. I used it at schools from then on, and in the Army, standing in ranks.

In the spring of my junior year at Fletcher, I had trouble not only with the Florida sand and heat but with the humidity, and I used to fall asleep in class.

When classes started, my trigonometry teacher was Edgar Holtsinger, who was also assistant football coach. Ed had played football for Georgia Tech; in fact, he was third team All-American there. He stood about six-foot-two and weighed about 225 pounds. His forearms looked like hams and his fingers looked like sausages and were at least an inch longer than mine.

Ed's teaching method was intimidation. I sat near the back row. He wore a size thirteen shoe, and when he came lumbering down the aisle, the floor squeaked, and his long arms and massive hands looked like they reached almost to his knees. I was scared to go to sleep in his class because if he caught anybody sleeping or nodding, he'd throw an eraser at them as hard as he could and knock hell out of them. I had a feeling I was going to have trouble with Ed because I thought Newboy training would offend him.

After I'd been in his class for several months, one morning a book fell and hit flat on the floor, and made a tremendous noise. It fell right next to where I was sitting. Everyone else jumped, but I didn't move a muscle or flinch, because of Newboy training. I saw Big Ed looking at me.

Sure enough, about a week later, the class was taking a

test, and Ed was walking up and down the aisles of the classroom. We were sitting in wood desks that were attached in rows, and Ed slipped up behind me with a yardstick. He took that yardstick and hit it flat on the desk behind me as hard as he could, and it sounded like a shotgun had gone off in the room. Everybody in the room jumped slap through the ceiling, but again, I didn't move a muscle or flinch.

I turned around slowly, almost as a reflex without thinking, and looked up at Ed and asked, "What time is it?" From that time on, Ed and I developed a rapport that would help me the rest of the year, and indeed was instrumental in my passing trigonometry at Fletcher.

I stayed awake in Ed's class, but I had particular trouble with the period after lunch, a study hall with Miss Humes.

I'd go in there after lunch and go to sleep. And she'd come back to my desk and raise hell. I had my head on my desk and my arms stretched out, and she'd pull on my arms and tell me "Wake up! You are here to study!" Then she'd turn around and go back to her desk and before she'd get back to her desk, I'd be asleep again. Miss Humes had told me that if I didn't straighten up, she was going to talk to my parents.

Around Easter, Brother came home from Western Kentucky. He was nineteen. I put Brother in one of Pa's suits, he put on Pa's hat, and he went over to Fletcher. I told Miss Humes that my father wanted to talk to her. She said fine, she wanted to talk to him. Brother knocked on her door after school and introduced himself as my father. He fooled her completely; she thought he was my father, and she told him how I had misbehaved at school. He said he didn't understand that, because Herby was a good boy around the house and helped his wife with the dishes and did what he was told. But he assured her that he would get the situation straightened out. He talked to her about twenty minutes. I waited outside the school. And when he left the room, he thanked Miss Humes, and asked her to have patience with me and assured her that my behavior would improve. He was walking down the hall in Pa's suit, had Pa's hat in his hand, and in the hall he passed the coach, whose name was Ish Brant.

He spoke to Ish, and it just so happened that after we left, Ish asked Miss Humes, "Who was that?" And she said "Oh, that was Herby's father. We just had a good talk." And Ish said, "Well, I don't know who that was, but that wasn't Herby's father."

So there was much trouble. They found out who that was, and Miss Humes was fit to be tied. The next morning when I came to school I saw Ed Holtsinger waving from 'way down the end of the hall, to come down there. This was before school started. He said "You are in a lot of trouble." I said "Not any more. I got Pa down here yesterday and got everything straightened out." And he said, "They know! They know!" And he said "They're having a meeting this morning, of all your teachers, and they're going to expel you from school."

Well, some of the teachers did vote to expel me, others didn't. They took me into the principal's office and lectured to me. And they called Mother and told her what had happened. They agreed that I could stay in school, but I was on probation, and if I did anything to cause more trouble they were going to expel me. When they called Mother, Mother cried, and told Pa about it. Pa didn't give a damn one way or the other. It was typical of Pa not to get excited about the incident. I stayed there the rest of the year.

Pa's reaction to that incident, as in so many others in my childhood and high school years, was consistent with Pa's openly detached viewpoint on life and total lack of concern for what others thought. I believe that through reading the works of Dr. Ken Cooper on exercise, I have come to understand the source of Pa's attitude about life.

I have been a long time admirer of Dr. Cooper, who runs the Cooper Clinic in Dallas, Texas. I've read all the books by Dr. Cooper, who is really the father of aerobics in this country. He came to Jacksonville for a lecture and I got a chance to talk to him one-on-one. I've been quite a student of exercise and fitness, all my life. Dr. Cooper fascinates me because he's got all these theories, and I think they're right.

After one of his lectures, I asked Dr. Cooper if a man was fifty years old and had never exercised nor was physically active would he get in shape as fast as a man who was physically fit at twenty but had been inactive and unfit from the time he was twenty until he was fifty.

Dr. Cooper said there was no medical answer for that question, but a man who had exercised as a young man would get in shape faster because the body remembers.

Later I received further proof of that statement through conversations with Byron Fuller, a friend of mine who lives in Ponte Vedra. He had been a Navy pilot. He was shot down over North Vietnam when he was 39 years old. At that time, Byron was a strapping six-footer who weighed 170 pounds. He remained a prisoner-of-war for more than six years.

During his imprisonment, much of which was spent in solitary confinement, he endured the worst living conditions imaginable, including torture, extended periods of being exposed to cold temperatures and a near-starvation diet. He was near death several times and at one time weighed less than 100 pounds.

Upon his return in 1973, he regained his health and went back up to his original 170 pounds. He ran in several River Runs in the mid-1980s. His pace in these races was about nine minutes, which is very close to what he could have done had he not gone to Vietnam.

The human body can survive, recover, come back and it can remember. It also has spare parts including two eyes, two ears, two kidneys, etc., and it can sustain life at about one seventh of its capacity. In other words it can operate on about one seventh of its power. All of this speaks clearly that the human body is an amazing machine.

When I went out to the Cooper Clinic, I went for the specific purpose of seeing if I should slow down on my exercising, because I was exercising about eight to ten hours a week now. He said whatever I was doing, don't change it, because I was in the 99 percentile of my age group.

When he came to Jacksonville to lecture, Dr. Cooper said something I thought applied to Pa. Pa would never have joined Brother and me in any physical activity, because he never did anything that involved exercise.

Dr. Cooper said that exercise now is the "in" thing to do all over the world, and that he gave lectures in different countries, in China, and Europe, but there was one country that had not taken to exercise. Although they go to lectures and hear the talk and have the research, and don't say it's wrong, they just don't do it; and that's England.

The English people will not exercise. Pa's ancestors were from England, and Pa would not exercise, period. He didn't run. He didn't do calisthenics. I never saw him do any manual labor. His comfort was his main objective, every day, all day. When he got in his car he'd have the air conditioner wide open, and he would never do anything to jeopardize his comfort at any time. The English people are like that.

I visited England one time. They go to church on Sunday morning, but they don't go home after church, they go right to the pub, and they drink, and they will not exercise, and that's right where Pa was. It's amazing that Pa got along as well as he did, because he defied everything we know about health today. He overate, and ate red meat whenever he could get it. He drank too much. He smoked two packs of cigarettes a day for over sixty years, starting when he was sixteen years old. He was overweight, would not exercise, and yet he was healthy, lived until he was seventy-nine years old, and died of a heart attack. But he was tough as hell; he had to be.

This lifestyle applied not only to Pa, but to that post-war generation of businessmen. They defied all we know about health and nutrition today. But they were hearty men who worked like hell.

Pa had a way about him of saying everything exactly as it was; there was never any doubt about where he stood on any issue. One of his strong traits was that he had great instincts. He could make major decisions fast and was usually right.

You might say, "Well, you know, he wasn't a very good father." But the opposite was true, because Pa taught me at an early age that I was on my own.

I can remember I used to go up and see Pa in the mountains. When Pa was in his sixties, he quit work and moved to the North Carolina mountains. He built a little frame house in Linville, and we've still got the house today.

Whenever I visited, Pa and I got up every morning about five o'clock and drank coffee on the back porch.

During those talks I came to appreciate that Pa was an excellent conversationalist. He'd talk about business and about life, and I always looked forward to talking to him, because he had very fixed opinions on everything. He didn't worry about the things most people worry about. He would not object to anything you wanted to do or anywhere you wanted to go. It was fine with him as long as he didn't do it. In other words, if you wanted to jump off a cliff, he'd take you over to the edge and let you out.

I remember one time—it must have been about twenty years ago, I guess—I had a twenty-five-foot wore-out sailboat, the River Rat II, named after our riverboat. My parents knew that Mitchell Rhodes and I were planning to sail from Jacksonville up the St. Johns River from my house to the ocean and up the coast to Charleston, S. C. They also knew that I'd never done any ocean sailing and that my boat wasn't very big. The day we went out, there were tornado warnings up, and a storm covered the entire southeast.

Mother and Pa were up in the mountains. I was leaving on a Friday; Mother had watched the weather and knew about this whole massive storm. She called to see that I didn't go because the weather was bad. But of course, I had gone, and Mother worried herself to death, and couldn't sleep because she knew I was out in that ocean in a big storm.

Later, Mother told me there was thunder and lightning in the mountains that night; they had never had such violent weather; and she didn't sleep well, worrying about me down on the ocean. And Pa came in the next morning and Mother was just fretting and said, "Did you sleep at all?" Pa said yeah, he slept fine—he thought he was going to have a little indigestion after supper, but he didn't, and had a good night's sleep. Pa didn't worry about other folks.

Pa finally did get sick; he had a heart attack. I had to take him to the doctor periodically and to the hospital. We'd go to Memorial Hospital, usually, or to St. Vincent's, and we'd go up to the desk to check in and he'd give them his name and address. They would say, "What religion are you?" and he wouldn't answer, and then they'd say, "Where do you go to church?" and he wouldn't answer. I finally told him, "Pa, dammit, tell them something. I don't care what you tell them, but you make up an answer before we get there."

He'd be sick as a yard dog and we'd be anxious to get him in his room, and he'd do fine with the questions up until those questions. Then he wouldn't answer, he'd just look. Which was typical for Pa. Pa would always keep you at arm's length, everybody; and if you'd get talking about something that was too personal or too private, he wouldn't say, "Well, I don't want to talk about that," and he wouldn't give you an off-the-wall answer. He just wouldn't answer at all. He'd just look at you.

At the hospital, I'd just say, "He's Baptist; he goes to whichever one is open." But he wouldn't answer them at all, because he didn't go!

While I was at Fletcher High School, Pa decided it had come time for him to have a Lincoln automobile. He bought a black 1949 Lincoln; it cost $3,600 and consumed almost all of the family resources and cost about a third as much as the house we were living in. There was a problem with the Lincoln—it would not fit in the garage. Our house was up on a little rise, and the Lincoln stuck out of the garage from the back door handles back. Everybody rode down First

Street and when I got to school, I got a bunch of kidding about whose car that was. It embarrassed the hell out of me, and I went home and told Pa the damn car was too big for the garage and it was embarrassing. His answer was that it was the garage's fault, not the car's.

In the summers before and after my year at Fletcher, I worked in a service station. Pa was working for Billups. I went to Orlando, and Brother went to Pensacola, and we worked in Billups stations.

In those days, there were no canopies. We worked six and a half days a week out in the weather, and we worked twelve-hour shifts. During that twelve hours you were not supposed to sit down. Billups sold a lot of tires and seat covers, and we were doing manual labor out in the sun, changing tires and installing seat covers. It was extremely tough. I know that seems hard to imagine, but that's the way it was. I made $35 a week.

I rented a room, and ate at a restaurant. I think the first summer, I worked for a month. In spite of all the hardship, I liked it; I met a lot of people, and I was outdoors; it was physical.

When basketball season started at Fletcher, I went out for the team. Just like back in Kentucky, I could stand outside around the foul circle and hit consistently, which no one else on the team could do. At that stage I just happened to be a better basketball player than the Florida boys because I had played more. Living in Kentucky, I had been playing basketball the year around, and the Florida boys had not. Fletcher's coach was Scotty Henderson, and he was very impressed.

Even though Newboy was unknown at the school, I made the first team. I started at guard. Brother was home on

Christmas vacation from Western Kentucky when we played our first game. We played Landon High School, one of Jacksonville's largest, in their gym on the Southside. Our whole family went to the game, and I went in with the team. The crowd packed the gym. When I came in to warm up I could see Pa and Brother and Mother and Sister sitting on the back row.

I remember the night very clearly, and that was in December 1948 and I was sixteen years old. We got the tip-off, and we came down the court and when I got the ball out beyond the foul circle, I faked a pass to the guard on the other side and ran in for a lay-up, and scored the first two points of the game.

They got the ball and went down and scored. I came back and got the ball again at the same place, faked again and ran down and this time I didn't go up for a lay-up, but I ran down the side of the court about six feet to the right of the goal and shot a hook shot. It went up there and bobbed around and went in.

They went down and scored again; then the score was 4 to 4. We came back down the court and I faked like I was going in and stopped and shot a one-handed shot from about the foul circle and it hit the bottom of the net, and we were ahead 6 to 4.

The whole gym went wild. The Landon coach called time out, and as I walked to the bench I looked up in the stands, and of course all the Fletcher fans including my family were on their feet and cheering, except Pa.

Pa was sitting there quiet and still, looking straight ahead. Now it wasn't that Pa wasn't excited; it wasn't that he wasn't proud of me; but Pa really thought that's what I should have been doing anyway.

They went on to beat us, but I was high point man of the game and from that point on I was not Newboy. At Fletcher, all of a sudden everybody knew me, and I really felt at home. I settled in and liked Fletcher very much. It was a good school. I liked the people at the beach, and that was a good year.

Shortly before Pa died, I was sitting on his back porch with him up in the mountains, and asked him where he wanted to be buried. He said he didn't care, because he wouldn't be there anyway. He did not elaborate on where he thought he would be, or on what basis he would get there. However, it is hard for me to worry much about that, because I know Pa is looking out for his own self.

On June 21, 1981, Pa had another heart attack and died. I've missed him much more than I ever thought I would. He had the unusual trait of looking at you straight in the eye and telling you exactly what he thought, both barrels, on all matters. He was so direct and so genuine. I loved him.

I can remember the first time I ever rode down to Ponte Vedra, not long after I came to Florida. Pa drove our family down there one Sunday in his red '47 Dodge. And I can remember the impression the Ponte Vedra Inn and Club made on me. There was nothing like that in Kentucky. The Inn looked very much like it does today. There were just a few rooms on the ocean side of the highway, but the Surf Club was there, along with the Racquet Club and, of course, the golf course.

I can remember thinking that was the most beautiful place I had ever seen. Of course we were never members and I never had an occasion to visit down there, but I used to drive down there, just to look.

It seemed to me the grass was greener in Ponte Vedra

than anywhere else in Florida. One time I walked into the tile roofed Inn. It was breathtaking, it was so beautiful, with its high-beamed ceilings and polished hardwood floors.

If, at that time, they had lined everybody up in the back of the gym at Fletcher High School, and said, "Alright now, we are going to pick out the person who will own the Ponte Vedra Inn and Club thirty-five years down the road," I would have been absolutely the last one they would have picked. If somebody had told me that was going to happen later in life to me, I could not even have imagined it.

We had a lot of sharp people at Fletcher High School, good students, fine families and good athletes. The fact that I, instead of one of those beach families, wound up owning Ponte Vedra, follows an unbelievable sequence of events that can only happen in America.

— Chapter Five —

Colorado

The summer between my junior and senior years, my family went to Colorado to visit my father's brother Ben. He lived out in the mountains fifty miles west of Denver in a town called Evergreen. We were on vacation there for a week, and had a great time. Ben made the mistake of saying, "Why don't you let Herby stay out here and go to school this year?"

Well, if you ever said that to Pa you better mean it, because he'd damn sure take you up on it. So come September I found myself on a train headed for Denver, Colorado, to spend my senior year of high school.

Brother was still in Bowling Green and going to Western Kentucky University. I enrolled in Evergreen High School, a small country high school way up in the mountains, attended mostly by the children of ranchers and farmers. There were eighteen in my graduating class. I developed some close friends out there. I lived with my uncle, played on the football and basketball teams, graduated there in June 1950, and came back to Florida.

In Colorado, because of the extreme weather, the schools are heated and air conditioned. You could never raise the windows. When I got out there, I was Newboy again, and I hadn't been there very long until I sat over by a radiator built into the wall. I would whistle, and hit the radiator with a book, and the whistling would stop. Of course, since I was the Newboy, nobody in the room knew what was going on, and they had the maintenance people come in there and take the whole thing apart, even while class was going on.

And they got it all put back together, and as they were leaving the room, they got halfway to the door, and I whistled again. And it caused much unhappiness. I did that on and off the whole year I was out there, and I never was suspected.

The elevation was about 7,500 feet. We used to play football against Denver high schools; they were only a mile high. They'd come up to Evergreen and the lack of oxygen would really work on them. Our game plan was always the same, to run them in the first half as much as we could, up and down the field. It worked, sometimes; in the second half we beat them.

My football playing was fair in Colorado; I was the first team end on offense and defense. We played both ways then. I could catch a pass, and they threw the ball to me several times every game. I was a pretty good broken field runner after I caught the ball, so I did better at football out there than I had ever done. I had a pretty good background in basketball after playing in Kentucky and Florida, and I did pretty well in basketball, too.

I remember one time we had a rival basketball game with the town of Idaho Springs. We went to play on their court in this little town about thirty miles up the road in the mountains. They told me that it was such a rivalry that when the teams came out and warmed up, instead of practicing lay-ups and shots, they'd shadowbox. The rivalry was more intense than anything in Kentucky. We got about twenty points behind in the last quarter. Everybody was as mad as hell, so when one of their players got the ball and headed down center court, I tackled him. I got up and he had trouble walking. They blew the whistle and the

coach came out on the floor and they were going to throw
me out, and I told them I slipped.

They started the game again and the next time — this
was the last two minutes — they got the ball and a boy on
their team started down the sidelines, dribbling, and I came
and body blocked him and knocked him four rows up in
the bleachers. Several of our players, including me, were
thrown out of the game. Our coach, his name was
Campbell, raised hell in the locker room about how we got
the hell beat out of us. And I can remember him saying,
"Peyton, what you did, that didn't help matters either."

When Idaho Springs came back to play in our gym, later,
we beat them by one point in overtime. Because of what had
happened in the earlier game I was not allowed to start. But
I came in and played a good game and we won.

I really did have some good times out there. My uncle
was living in a small house with his wife, Nell, and a
daughter, Ann, who was my age and in my class. Uncle was
not a rancher, he was retired. He had served in World War I
in France and gotten tuberculosis, and was on a partial
disability pension from the Army. They had said that he
should live at a high altitude, and that's why he went out to
Colorado. They were real good to me, and I loved being
with them. Ben died later of a brain tumor, then Aunt Nell
died, and Ann has died. I never did see any of them again.

Being in Colorado for nine months was like a prolonged
vacation. Uncle made me a part of his family. I developed a
great love for the state of Colorado and for the West in
general. Those people seem to have a great love and respect
for nature and the out-of-doors. I could not have picked a
better place to spend my senior year of high school.

I still go out West every chance I get. For many years

now I have been taking my family to Colorado skiing. We have a great time and look forward to it every year.

My senior year, I came home to Florida for Christmas by way of Kentucky. I rode a Greyhound bus thirty-six hours from Denver to Bowling Green. Brother was still there going to college, and I got to see all my old friends that I had been away from for a couple of years. When Brother and I were traveling we had two missions: one was to travel for free, and the other was to try to beat the bus schedule. We usually could do both. This time we rode a freight train from Bowling Green to Florida.

I called the freight yard to see when their next freight was going to Nashville. They said one would pull out about eleven o'clock that night. A carload of the boys—Bob Dickey, Hugh David Roe, Jay Bettersworth, and others—drove Brother and me down there, and sure enough, between eleven and midnight the freight train started up and pulled out, heading south. We bade our friends farewell and swung up on the train.

The most dangerous part of riding freight trains is getting on and off. If you try to swing up on one that is going faster than you are it'll pull you under the train and cut your legs off. So Brother and I had found out early, when you are riding freight trains, you've got to get running the same speed the train is going before you grab on and swing up. If you don't you're in trouble.

So we would always catch the freight train just as it was pulling out, going five or six miles an hour, so we could run alongside and get going the same speed. You couldn't go into the freight yard to get on the train because they had yard detectives there and they'd raise hell, so what you did was wait outside the freight yard. You knew which train it was, and as it pulled out you would swing up on it.

We got into Nashville about three o'clock in the morning. We made the same inquiries about when the next train was heading south to Chattanooga. The people working on the freight trains in Nashville told us, "Well, this train here's going to Chattanooga, and it'll be a couple of hours." We went out of the yard and waited, and about daylight it pulled out, and we swung on.

We found out that there were different kinds of accommodations on freight trains. The coal cars were not very comfortable on top, but they had a slanted bottom, and you could ride up under the car where the wheels were, in an angled space where you could sit.

Of course, the best accommodations were boxcars. Most of the time the boxcars were locked, and it was not easy to get in while the train was moving. It was much easier getting up on the end where the ladders were. When we could find an open boxcar we'd get in there and be very comfortable, out of the wind and the weather. That was luxury accommodations. Brother could sleep while we were riding along. We did have to ride on top of coal cars sometimes, which was the worst of accommodations.

I remember one time we were riding up under a coal car, in the slanted area above the wheels. Brother had the ability to make himself at home, no matter where he was or what the circumstances were, even on a freight train. We carried all our stuff in a duffel bag when we were traveling on the freight train, and we also had a machete. I never did understand why we carried the machete, but I guess that was the closest thing we had to defense. Brother carried a machete most places he went, to the woods or the river or on a trip. He never carried a gun on our trips, but he did carry a machete, in a holster. Under the coal car, he was sharpening his machete on the wheels, and the sparks were flying out and hitting his hand and he was slapping at them. And I told him to put that damn machete away and sit there quiet, and he did.

So we went from Nashville to Chattanooga, and from Chattanooga to Atlanta. Atlanta was very tough because it was such a large freight yard. We had heard they had police out there and would put you in jail if they caught you. We had trouble, but we finally did get on a train going out of Atlanta and rode to Jacksonville.

While Brother was still a junior at Western Kentucky, he had become interested in boxing. He took boxing in gym class and boxed around Bowling Green a little bit. He got pretty good, or he thought he was pretty good, and he got some coaching and decided to get in the Golden Gloves tournament.

The place to get in the Golden Gloves was Nashville, Tennessee, sixty-five miles down the road. I did not attend since I was in Colorado, but I heard all about it. Brother went down there and fought as a welterweight, 147 pounds. When he got down there, it just so happened that through the tournament draw he fought against the boy who had won it the year before, which meant he was much more experienced than Brother.

When Brother entered the ring in the Nashville arena, he came out in a bathing suit and tennis shoes with a towel around his neck. His opponent presented himself in red silk shorts and a red silk robe, and was dancing in his corner of the ring when Brother slid through the ropes.

There was another problem: the boy he fought was left-handed. Brother had never before fought a left-handed fighter, and he didn't know his opponent was left-handed until the fight started. His opponent lined up exactly opposite from what he was supposed to, and before Brother figured out he was left-handed, he had knocked Brother down three times in the first round.

Pa had driven up there for the fight, and was sitting on the back row of the gym. And when Brother got knocked down, Pa got out in the aisle and lumbered down to the ring. By this time, Brother was semiconscious, bloody and lying on his back near the edge of the ring, and Pa was hollering at the top of his voice in Brother's ear, "Get up, Genz!"

But anyway, Brother got beat up pretty bad. He lasted less than two minutes. Thus ended Brother's boxing career.

Brother's plan was to get a degree in agriculture and become a Kentucky farmer, which he should have been, because he would have been a natural. That was a good plan, but it didn't work. And the reason it didn't work was that he came home after his junior year and announced at the supper table that he was going to need five years to graduate instead of four, which meant he had two more years of college. He was taking ROTC, which required him to get behind in his other subjects, and he was shy of credits for graduation.

Well, that didn't set too well with Pa. As a matter of fact, Pa said that enough was enough, and he wasn't going to finance any more college. Pa said, "The hell with that! You're going in the Army now. You've been up there too damn long anyway, and that's money down a rat hole." That was in the summer of 1950 and the Korean War was heating up. So Brother joined the Air Force. He went to Lackland Air Force Base for basic training and wound up in pilot school and became a jet fighter pilot. He went to Korea for a year, but by the time he got there, the fighting was about over. He did some patrolling, but was never in actual combat.

I graduated from Evergreen High School in June, and came home to Florida. During my twelve years of school I had attended ten schools in four states: Kentucky, Tennessee, Florida, and Colorado. For five of those twelve years, I had lived away from home with relatives.

Shortly after I returned to Florida from Colorado, the Korean War broke out. I registered for the draft and then I decided to go into the Army on the volunteer inductee program, which meant instead of waiting to get drafted, you went early. But you had the same status as a draftee, you were just in for two years.

While I was waiting to report, I went to Jacksonville University during its first year out at the new Arlington campus, until I left for the Army in January, right after Christmas.

When I left that night on the train, it wasn't a freight train; I rode like decent people up to Columbia, South Carolina, on a passenger train to report to Fort Jackson. The family went to Union Station in Jacksonville about dark that night in Pa's car.

When I left, the Chinese were massing on the Korean border, fixing to come into North Korea, and there was talk about World War III, and heavy casualties were expected, and everything looked bleak. Pa listened to the news going into town, and Mother started to cry because she thought I was going to go over there and the Chinese were going to kill me. Now this was typical of Pa: he didn't worry about that; he was concerned that we were going to be late for the train.

—Chapter Six—

The Army Calls

I got up to Columbia, South Carolina, at two o'clock in the morning. A sergeant met us at the train in an Army truck and took us out to Fort Jackson. When we got there, we stood in line in eighteen degree cold during processing, until about seven or eight o'clock in the morning, while they issued us field jackets and fatigues. Of course, I didn't have on enough clothes; nobody did.

Fort Jackson was running over with troops. They were beefing up the Army, getting ready for the Korean War. I stayed there for the standard basic training course. It was tough as hell.

We had a master sergeant named Anderson. He was a typical regular army sergeant with a long WWII combat record. One particular day he hurried me all day. I finally told him that if he wouldn't rush me, I would work cheaper. He told me that I was making $52 a month, which was the least I could make in the Army and he assured me that I was not being underpaid.

Back then, the discipline was strict. I could whistle in ranks, and it would just cause an uproar. There would be a mean drill sergeant out there barking, "Company, atten-hut!" And then I whistled right after he gave that command. And he would go absolutely berserk. I had never heard such threats and foul language as they used, and I don't guess they had ever heard anything like that noise in the Army before, either. I transferred a lot in the Army, and I created turmoil on every base I went to. And of course, I got better—even louder and more shrill. And I did have a hell of a time with it.

While I was in the Army my whistle really became quite famous, because they couldn't even start to tell where it was coming from. It was a piercing, ringing, irritating noise; they didn't even call it a whistle. They'd say, "Who's making that noise?" And the thing about it was that I could do it with my mouth just barely open, standing at attention. I was never accused of making that noise because they could look at me and see I wasn't whistling. I had perfected my poker face in the pup tent in Bowling Green long before the tonsillectomy created my motionless whistle. And of course, Newboy training was very helpful in this regard.

Once I whistled at Fort Bragg, and a sergeant who lived off base went home and told his wife about this noise in ranks, and how they couldn't find out who it was, and it was driving everybody crazy. His wife worked with the wife of an Air Force man who had been stationed with Brother at Lackland Air Force Base, Texas, one thousand miles away.

The sergeant's wife told the Air Force wife from Texas about the whistle and the Air Force wife mentioned it to her husband. That Air Force sergeant came over to the barracks one night, and looked me up, and said, "I know about that whistle." He said, "I was stationed with your brother in Texas, and he told me about that whistle." He said, "I knew when I heard about it that it had to be you." He and his wife kept quiet, but that was the closest I ever came to getting caught.

On a visit home from the Army, I decided to go back to the well-known doctor, Dr. Marshall Taylor, who had taken out my tonsils. I told him, "I've got something peculiar about my throat, and you took my tonsils out, and I'd like you to look at it." I went into his office, and he acted like he was kind of bored, and he said, "What is it?" And then I whistled.

And he thought I had something in my hand. He opened up both hands to see, and he really couldn't believe it. He was shocked. After much examination, he wanted me to go with him to the American Medical Association meeting, which was held in Miami that year, to show the other doctors.

Of course, I was in the Army and I couldn't get to the American Medical Association meeting or anywhere else. And I never did go with him. He never was able to explain what happened, and nobody else has explained it either, and I've never met anybody else in my life who has a whistle anything like mine.

I was in the Army two years. Under the volunteer induction program, you had about the same status as a draftee, and had trouble specifying what branch of the Army you wanted. I had tried to get into the paratroopers from basic training and it was hard to do. I was very lucky to get in at all, because they wanted people who were going to be in the Army for a long period of time. I went to Fort Bragg, North Carolina, and was assigned to the 82nd Airborne Division, and then I waited to go from there to jump school at Fort Benning, Georgia.

Jump school lasted three weeks and was one of the hardest periods of my life. We jumped five times at jump school. During that three weeks about forty percent of the class washed out.

I'll always remember our first day there; they lined us up in formation and the sergeant said, "Look to the right;

look to the left. I promise you one of you three will not be here in three weeks."

We never walked. The whole time I was there we ran everywhere we went. Of course, it was August and September, and in southern Georgia, inland, it was hot. I can remember coming back into the barracks at nine or ten o'clock at night, with rings of salt accumulated all over my fatigues. We stayed wringing wet with sweat all day, doing calisthenics and running. We must have done a thousand pushups a day.

When we finally did get back to the barracks at night, we lined up to go in the mess hall. There was a pull-up bar right before you went through the door to the mess hall, and there was a sergeant standing beside it. Everyone had to do ten pull-ups before he ate. If you did eight or nine or any lesser number, no food. Of course, you had the option, if you didn't want to do the pull-ups—no food.

During training, anybody who couldn't keep up, or passed out, or couldn't handle height, would be pulled out of ranks and sent back to the barracks. When we got there that night, his bunk mattress would be rolled up and he would be gone. You never knew where they went, but they got them out of there fast.

We did a lot of parachute landing falls they called PLFs. In a PLF, you jump off a four foot platform and land on your feet, and go into a roll where most of the shock is absorbed by your upper body. The first test of the ability to handle height was from a thirty-two foot tower. We would walk up these steps and get into the jump position and jump out without a parachute. We were in a parachute harness and free fell about twenty-five feet before being caught by a cable, just before hitting the ground. We slid down a cable about one or two hundred feet to a berm on the ground, where we got off.

Of course, some soldiers couldn't do that. They'd get up there and freeze, and when they did that, that was the end of it, they'd get them out of there. It was always a surprise as to who could do that and who couldn't. Some of the toughest and most fit and athletic boys would be the very ones who couldn't handle the height.

I remember we had our steel helmets on, with our name right across the front on white tape. Sergeants down below gave the command to jump. I remember it was hot as hell and I was just dragging and scared to death. I jumped that first time and when that cable stopped, it damn near knocked the wind out of me.

I got down there and stood by the pulley, and this great big sergeant is screaming in my ear, "How did you like that, Peyton?" And I said, "Well, I didn't like it so hot," and he said, "Well, get up there and do it again." And we did that all day for several days. More people washed out on the thirty-two-foot tower than in any other part of jump school.

The next training exercise was from a three hundred foot tower. We were hooked in a parachute in this harness, and they pulled us up just like an elevator, then we were released. With loud speakers they would instruct us how to guide the parachutes. They would say, "Pull to the right!" and so on.

There were two weeks of that kind of training, and the last week we jumped, once a day for five days, and graduated that Friday afternoon. So our first jump from an airplane was on Monday morning. I was nineteen years old, and I had never been up in an airplane. The first plane I ever went up in was a C-47, and I jumped out of it.

When I got up in that airplane, and they opened that door, the jumpmaster looked out the door for the drop zone and his skin folded back from the wind. I was literally scared to death. The flow of adrenaline put the taste of brass in my mouth. When I stepped out that door I thought the end had come.

They have different drop zones to allow for the wind and conditions. The second day, after we started jumping, they decided the wind was blowing in a different direction than they had thought. They tried to stop our jump, so they could reposition the plane and get more allowance for wind. The jumpmaster stepped in front of us and tried to get us to stop.

By that time, we were all so scared he couldn't stop us. The whole damn line of paratroopers, the "stick," ran out the door. We were too psyched up and too excited to be stopped. In the Army, the closest I ever came to combat was stepping out the door of that airplane, and that was very similar to what I think combat would be like.

I was extremely motivated. I wanted to be a paratrooper more than anything I'd ever wanted in my life, and I went all out. I graduated on that Friday, and got orders to go back to Fort Bragg. When I got back there, I thought my next stop was Korea. I had completed my training—I was no longer a straightleg, and I was ready.

I told the First Sergeant that I was ready to go, and he said, "Go where?" I said, "Well, hell, I'm going to Korea. That's the reason I joined the Army." He said, "You're not going anywhere. You're in the 82nd."

The 82nd at that time was the National Honor Guard, which meant they were the only division kept on alert at all times and at full strength, so you couldn't transfer in or out.

So I decided to go to see the division commander.

I went up to his office and told the sergeant that I wanted to see the division commander. I think they were surprised that I'd come in like that. He said, "Wait just a minute, I'll see," In a few minutes I was shown into the office of a Brigadier General who was Assistant Division Commander. And I went in there and saluted and told him that I was Private Peyton and that I had been trained, and I joined the Army to go to Korea, and my training was through and I was ready.

He said, "Well, you're in the 82nd, we'll see about that." So I left his office and he wrote down what outfit I was in. On the way back to the company I happened to go by the chapel, and chaplain was there, so I went in and told him how badly I wanted to go to Korea, and I wanted his help.

Later that afternoon, they called a company formation, which was highly unusual in late afternoon. The company commander got out there and said, "I understand some of you people have been visiting the general and the chaplain about transferring out. You're not transferring anywhere. Not only that, you haven't got time to go visiting like that, and if there is any more of that there's going to be a lot of trouble."

Before he dismissed the formation, he said, "I want Private Payton to report to my office immediately following this formation." He got me down there in that office and he was in a rage. "Let me tell you one damn thing: you just got in this outfit. I don't want you ever in my office again, and if you ever go ask anybody about going to Korea again, or anywhere else, I promise you I'll personally court-martial you, and you'll go to the stockade." He said, "I don't want to hear anymore about you. Get back in your barracks and go to work and keep quiet."

Later, I tried to get on some athletic teams. I tried out for the boxing team, but after about a week and many licks, I figured out that a big head and short arms is not a good combination for a boxer. I went out for the division football team; didn't make that either.

A lot of the paratroopers were veterans of World War II, and of the Normandy jump and the Holland jump. Most had tattoos, and they were really rough guys. When I first went up there, I lived in a barracks with about fifty soldiers. They had one gang shower, and I remember them questioning me when I first got there about when I was going to get tattooed. Most of them had the word paratroopers or images of parachutes on their arms.

I spent the remainder of my two years in the Army with the 82nd Airborne Division at Fort Bragg. These people were fine soldiers, and I was proud to be among them.

In my generation, we thought you should go to war for our country. I was in grammar school when World War II was being fought. I, and everybody in my generation, felt that we should go in the service because the country needed us. I felt I should not only go to the Army, but I should be fighting; I just believed that was my duty, and that's where I wanted to be. There was never any question about it.

I really do believe if I'd ever gotten to Korea—and God knows I tried— one of two things would have happened. I'd either have gotten killed or gotten some medals. And if I'd gotten some medals, I'd have stayed in the Army, and I'd be retired right now. I liked the regimentation and the camaraderie and the physical part of it, and I was very proud of being a paratrooper.

As a preliminary to the Officer's Candidate School, I

went to leadership school at Camp Gordon, in Augusta, Georgia. After that, I signed up for OCS, but by the time my application was processed and I could have been accepted, I was about six months from getting out of the Army. I would have had to reenlist for three additional years, and I said "No, to hell with that." By that time the Korean War was winding down, so I came home. The highest rank I achieved in the two years was Pfc—private first class.

I still like the Army. I have always had great respect for the military, and I would consider it more of an honor to have a combat infantryman's badge than to hold any university's diploma, with very few exceptions. Although I never did get to combat—and maybe I would feel differently if I had—I have great respect for those who did, and around an airport when I see a soldier wearing the combat infantry badge and several rows of ribbons, I am duly impressed.

My generation was too young for World War II, but I have always been proud of the fact that when the Korean War came, we stepped up.

These are the memories of a teenage soldier. With age I have mellowed; I am not as gung ho. This also explains why the Army prefers young soldiers.

—Chapter Seven—

Learning The Trade

I was honorably discharged from Fort Bragg in January
1953, when I was almost twenty-one years old. I went
home and almost the next day, the folks put me on a bus
going to Sewanee, Tennessee, to attend the University of the
South on the GI bill.

The Army had paid me $50 a month when I first went in,
and later I got jump pay of $100 plus my base pay. I used to
be in the loan shark business, loaning those boys $20 until
payday and getting back $30, so I had accumulated some
money.

When I got to college, I went down the road to Lebanon,
Tennessee, a little town south of Sewanee, and paid $1600
cash for my first car, a six-cylinder '53 Mainliner Ford. It
was trimmed in black rubber and had nothing on it but a
heater, a radio and a spare tire. It was a fine car and I kept it
for years; I wish I had it today.

I joined the SAE fraternity at Sewanee. I was Newboy
again, and I didn't know whether I could pass up there. It
was a very good school and academically my background
was not so hot. I really settled down and studied hard and
found out that I could pass. I made B's and C's, which was
damn good, for me. But I decided that I needed to take
business courses instead of Sewanee's liberal arts program.
Also, Sewanee was an all-boys school.

I was getting some age on me and thought it was time I
started trying to think of what I was going to do, so I
transferred to the University of Florida in September '53—
Newboy again—and lived in the fraternity house. The UF

enrollment was about 10,000. It was a good school and I studied like hell down there, and I passed. I made some lifelong friends.

Pa called me. He was coming through Gainesville and wanted to see me. I said, "Fine." I remember when he came I was studying over at the law library not far from the SAE house; I had left word where I was. This was after I had passed one semester and was beginning the second. I was kind of proud of myself because I was passing, and because I had gotten to know a lot of people; and I liked the school and being involved.

Pa came over to the library and it was real quiet there, so we went out and sat in a little anteroom. He got real close to me and he talked in a real low voice and he told me I was wasting his money and my time, and it was time for me to go to work.

By this time, January 1954, I was twenty-two years old. It's true I was a little bit older than most of the students. I told him no, I didn't want to quit school. But I thought about it a week or two and I did quit, and went home. But that was a mistake. I look back on it, and there was really no special reason for me to quit. I should have stayed in school, but I didn't. I went back to Jacksonville and went to work for the company Pa worked for, Billups Petroleum Company.

To understand the Billups company you must understand its culture. Billups was started during the Depression by the three Billups brothers in Mississippi. The people that worked for Billups were desperate for a job. It was an independent company, which meant they sold cheaper than the major oil companies. Their slogan was "Fill up with Billups." The way they exploited their labor was unbelievable. I had worked for them before, during the summer while I was in high school in Florida. Billups still worked people twelve hours a day, six-and-a-half days a week, and we were not allowed to sit down at the station during that twelve hours. Of course, we got time off to eat. There were no canopies to protect us from the weather back then, and no front door on the station because they kept them open twenty-four hours a day.

A lot of that time it was just like my summer jobs while I was at Fletcher High School. We were doing manual labor, like changing tires and putting on seat covers. Physically it was unbelievably tough to be always hot in summer, cold in winter, wet when it rained, and standing up all that time. Of course, I was in extremely good shape from the Army then and could take it pretty well. I became disenchanted with Billups because of all of this. Working for Billups was not a job. It was an ordeal. The one thing they had going for them was this fact: "The harder the ordeal, the stronger the bond." That experience strengthened the bond in future years between Gate Brothers who had once worked for Billups.

But during that period I really learned the fundamentals of service station business. I managed service stations for Billups and traveled a lot throughout the Southeast. I worked in Virginia for a year, and in the Carolinas a lot. I couldn't have made it later, without that background.

When Billups opened a new station, I would usually manage it; I was not married and could stay on the road most of the time, living in motels. This was in the mid-1950s. While I was managing an Ocala station, a rodeo came to town, and I signed up for the bull riding. I drew a Brahma bull named Big Sid.

In order to ride, I had to join the RCA (Rodeo Cowboys' Association). I told them my name was Red Peyton, from Evergreen, Colorado, which was where I had graduated from high school.

A rider was required to stay on the bull for eight seconds, which didn't sound like much of a problem; I could do anything for eight seconds. I remember getting up on him in the chute and he was snorting and kicking, and I thought, "I'm not going to do so hot." They have a rope around the bull and you wear gloves to try to hold onto that rope. And I remember the last thing I heard while I was tightening my grip on that rope and the bull was stomping and trying to climb the walls of the chute was, "Red Peyton is coming out of chute number four—all eyes on chute number four."

They opened the door and that damn bull ran out about twenty feet from the side of the chute and started turning to the right, and then, all of a sudden, seemed like in midair, he started turning to the left, and he did what they call "sunfishing," where they flash their belly up. He did that a couple of times, and the next thing I knew, I was flying through the air. I know I must have been ten feet off the ground. As soon as I hit the ground, on my back, I looked up, and when I got my eyes focusing again the first thing I saw was that bull charging me with his head about six inches off the ground.

He was about ten feet away from me, and I can remember thinking, "Well, this is it." There were no rocks in Florida like the one that had saved me in Nashville. I kind of hunkered down because I thought he was going to gore me. He got awfully close before a clown ran between me and the bull to distract him, and I got up and ran off.

Now that I was registered, I was a professional rodeo

rider and I could ride in all the rodeos. I figured my best chance in rodeoing was in riding bareback broncos rather than Brahma bulls that move inside their skins. So the next winter, I went into the Silver Spurs Rodeo in Kissimmee, the biggest rodeo in the state of Florida. There were several thousand people watching. Most of the riders were from out West, and all of them were real good riders. I remember I had a dapple gray horse, and he came out of the chute bucking up and down and I got thrown off. I was thrown clear of the horse, he kept on going, and I got up and walked off.

The difference was, a horse doesn't try to stomp you, and they don't try to come back and gore you after they'd thrown you. As a matter of fact, a horse will try not to kick you when you go down. I found out from those experiences there was a hell of a lot to that rodeo riding. It isn't something you just go out there and start doing. I couldn't win and I kind of got out of the notion.

My rodeo career was brief, but it was a thrill to hear over the loudspeaker, "Red Peyton is coming out of chute number four." That is the closest I ever came to a professional athletic career, and it was short-lived—about fourteen seconds, both rides together.

The gasoline business offered real promise. It was an immature industry at that time, making tremendous growth in Florida. I started planning to have my own service station. As a bachelor I was able to save by living on my expense account most of the time. I invested a little bit in the stock market; and I made a little money on real estate.

After working for several years, I decided the time had come to go into business for myself. So in the summer of 1960, when I was twenty-eight years old, I quit Billups.

Ma's oil painting of Newboy and Brother fishing in Kentucky

Newboy

The Peyton House at
1220 State Street,
Bowling Green,
Kentucky

Private First Class
Herbert H. Peyton,
82nd Airborne
Division, U.S. Army

The River Rat—1948
Brother and Newboy
on the front deck

Newboy riding Big Sid

Ma's oil painting of the first Gate Station at Moncrief and 45th

Ma's oil painting of Newboy and John on the Mandarin dock in 1966

Newboy

A modern Gate service station and Gate Food Post

Newboy in Linville Gorge

Climbing the Tetons in Jackson Hole, Wyoming

Biggie and Newboy at a camp site in northern Canada near the Arctic Circle

Newboy

The Peytons on a 1986 Colorado ski trip (left to right—Jennifer Gaines Peyton, Henry Hill Peyton, Herbert Hill Peyton and John Stephens Peyton)

The beautiful Ponte Vedra Inn and Club

Blount Island in Jacksonville, Florida

The Riverplace Tower on the Southbank of the St. Johns River

—Part Two—

— Chapter Eight —

The Battle of Moncrief

In the summer of 1960, I incorporated Gate Petroleum Company. While working for Billups I had accumulated about $20,000, and the company's first station cost $18,000 to construct. The first station was built on a back street where property was cheap; ground leased for $250 a month. That's how I wound up at Moncrief.

That triangular site at the fork of 45th Street and Moncrief was kind of a Times Square for the black community of Jacksonville. Almost everybody went by there. It was a good corner, and still is today. We have a new station out there run by Doc Walker, one of our veteran managers, and it does fine. Some of the longtime customers still greet me as "Mr. Gate." The Moncrief station will always be special.

Moncrief opened on September 9, 1960, and our volume of 40,000 gallons that first month was not high. But when it turned cold in December, we got an unexpected bonus. People came from blocks and lined up, thirty and forty deep on a cold day, while I filled their jugs with kerosene for heaters. Back then, we bought kerosene for about ten cents a gallon and sold it for 17.9 cents cash. None was charged and we had a ten-day "float." We could sell three or four thousand gallons of kerosene. My profit doubled to tripled almost overnight as soon as it got cold, and Moncrief was making $3,000 to $4,000 a month profit that first winter, in addition to my $100 per week salary. Back in 1960, that was a lot of money. Kerosene season was five months at the most, but during those months, we made hay.

It just so happened during those first winters in the early 1960s, we had unusually cold weather, and that had a lot to do with Gate's early success.

We sold about a thousand packs of cigarettes a day. We didn't make much money on them; we used them as a leader to get people in the station.

I was the manager of Moncrief a year and a half, through that first winter and the next summer and winter. I was there at 6 a.m., seven mornings a week, working from can to can't.

This was a very rough period for me physically. During that time I was whipped, robbed, and shot at. One afternoon, a .38 special nickel-plated revolver was held to my throat. I was up on my tiptoes, because the gunman was pressing pretty hard, and he told me not to move a muscle. I stood quiet and still.

In the winter of 1962, Billy Rhodes quit Billups and came to Gate. When he joined Gate, he was holding nothing but the Ten Commandments.

About 10:30 p.m. one Saturday night during the second winter there, after closing the Moncrief station, Billy and I put $1,700 in my car trunk and headed to the bank for a night deposit. We started down Moncrief Road and turned the corner onto Golfair Boulevard, which was then a dirt road. Ahead of us we saw a roadblock set up with three cars. There were five black men with guns in front of us, and they were shouting for us to stop.

I drove right up on the roadblock before I saw it, because I was coming around the corner. I was so startled that instead of stopping, I put my foot to the floorboard, drove into the ditch, spun around, somehow got around the cars and kept going. They opened fire, and they shot out the windows in my car. We could hear the bullets ricocheting around the inside of the car. Pieces of glass splattered all over us. Billy didn't say a word during this exchange. We kept going and decided not to go to the bank. We thought they would follow us and intercept us at the bank, so we got up on I-95 and headed for home.

On the way home, Billy started talking, and he said in a monotone, kind of like he was talking to himself, "My neighbor goes to work at eight o'clock in the morning and I go to work before daylight. My neighbor gets off at five o'clock in the afternoon, and gets off on the weekend; and I work till after dark seven days a week, can to can't; and my neighbor works in an air-conditioned office and I work outside in the cold in the winter and the heat in the summer; and my neighbor has never been shot at. "

I was concerned. I thought Billy was talking himself into quitting, so I said, "Now Billy, I'm glad your neighbor is doing well, but you've got to remember there is a big difference between you and your neighbor. You are at war, and he is not." Billy showed up for work the next morning like a soldier.

And when I presented myself at Moncrief at 6 a. m. that morning, one of the employees, Shag, was standing on the front porch grinning. He said, "The boys said you wouldn't show this morning." I smiled back and said, "Shag, you tell the boys I'll be here at 0600 every morning." We understood each other very well.

Several weeks later I asked one of the other employees, Junior Brown, what he thought about the roadblock. He hung his head and thought for a minute, and then he said, "You did as good as you could have did."

Billy not only came to work the morning after the

roadblock, he worked for Gate for the next thirty-one years. In December of 1993, he died of a heart attack. Billy Rhodes was a service station man deluxe. For over three decades, his job was building and running service stations. He was not only good at his job, he was totally emotionally involved and he loved it. In addition to that, Billy Rhodes was the best-liked man in the company.

In our lifetime we will probably never see a more complete service station man than was Billy Rhodes. Billy came along about the same time that service stations made it big in this country. After World War II, because of television and air conditioning, people no longer had time to visit with their neighbors and rock on their front porch. Because of this, the service station developed into a kind of social center. It was a place where you met and visited with neighbors you didn't often see. It was a place where you got updated on what was happening in your community.

In 1963, the manager at Moncrief got drunk on Christmas Eve and called me at home Saturday afternoon. I went out there to check him out and to put the money in the bank. After a dispute about the money, he invited me outside. Although he was half drunk, he was big enough and still sober enough to whip me. And then he left.

I remember I was invited down to St. Augustine for Christmas Eve dinner, where everybody was dressed up. I showed up late, with a black eye. One arm was scraped from the elbow halfway down to the wrist, and I had on a long sleeved shirt. My host was a prominent lawyer in St. Augustine and a gentleman, and I can never forget the look of dismay on his face when I unbuttoned my shirt and pulled my sleeve up over the elbow to see if it was still bleeding. I had come down there bloodied up, and he could never understand how I could come to Christmas dinner like that.

While managing Moncrief, and since, I have developed many friends out at Moncrief and feel as though I know them better than most people do. Moncrief residents have more tolerance for adversity than we do. They seem to roll with the punches and get along better than most people. The truth is, they are emotionally tougher than most everyone else—they've had to be. They are survivors.

I remember one of them got put in jail, I've forgotten what for, and called me from the "P. Farm" needing $60 bail. He told me if I could get him out he would never forget it, and all that. Anyway, I went out there and bailed him out. On the way back, he said he would get paid Friday at four o'clock and he would be in there by four-thirty to pay me the $60, and he thanked me. Come Friday he didn't show up. I eventually got the money, but I had to hound the hell out of him to get it, $10 at a time.

He just didn't see any urgent obligation to pay me back the money, and that's kind of the way they were. Also, I was surprised at the mortality rate out there. While I was there, several people got killed: either shot, cut in knife fights, or run over when they were drunk, and even today you go out there and ask about somebody that you knew and they don't say he died, they say, "Oh, he got killed ten years ago," just like they were an Army casualty on the front line.

Growing up in Kentucky I was used to unusual sayings and unique ways of putting things. But in Moncrief, they had a language all their own. It wouldn't be, "where do you live?" They would say, "where do you stay?" You wouldn't hear, "what did he do?" Instead, it would be a simple, "what he did?" Even though sometimes they had trouble with sentence structure and tenses, they had no trouble communicating. And although they sometimes expressed themselves differently, their meaning was very clear.

Back in those days, cigarettes cost a quarter, and their standard saying was "loan me a quarter out your pocket to buy some cigarettes." When I wouldn't loan them the money, another of their standard sayings was, "Oh, Mr. Gates, you knows I'll pay you back." They worked me over pretty good when I first got there, but after I had been there awhile I wised up.

Moncrief was rough, especially at night. I remember one Sunday morning, the phone inside the station was out of order, and I went outside to the phone booth. The booth had bullet holes in it and blood all over it. I got out of the notion to make the call. That community was like a combat zone.

Gate had no office. I ran the company from the service station, and I carried all the bills and gasoline invoices and the payroll information in an old leather satchel. Back in those days, I wasn't concerned with balance sheets or profit and loss statements. The real gauge of how we were doing was on payday; if I could pay everybody and have any money left over in the bank, I was doing pretty good. If I ran out of money, I wasn't doing so hot. That was a much better barometer than we have today.

It became obvious in the early days of Gate that the gasoline business had two unique features that made it possible to expand very fast. When gasoline was delivered to our stations, we had ten days to pay for it and usually the gas was sold within about three days. Therefore, we had a full week's float, or a negative inventory. In other words, we were operating on our supplier's money for at least a week, and as we got more stations and higher volume, this float increased. We still have it today, and it is a tremendous amount of money.

The other unique quality we have is that every day, we read our meters and stick our tanks, so we know every day whether we are short or over. This makes a damn good combination for expansion.

When I first managed Moncrief, I was still a bachelor, and I rented an apartment on River Road near the Fuller Warren Bridge. I'd get on the bridge, go right up I-95, and get off on Golfair and go to Moncrief. It took me about fifteen minutes to get up there, so that worked real well.

An old army friend of mine, Andy Sears, used to come out to see me once in awhile. Those were the days of segregation and we couldn't eat in black restaurants. We had to drive about two miles to eat lunch. Andy came out there, not because he enjoyed Moncrief. He came to see me because he knew I was having a tough time and needed his support. That was the kind of friend he was. Andy was my friend in the army, in college and in business for nearly fifty years. He recently died of cancer.

The years when I was out at Moncrief by myself were stressful years. I remember I went out and waited on a car, and the driver had gone to Fletcher High School with me. He was in the neighborhood on some kind of welfare work. He was quite shocked to see me there, and felt really sorry for me, tried to cheer me up and said not to get discouraged, he thought things would get better for me. He didn't know it, but I was doing fine. I thought I had the best job in town.

—Chapter Nine—

Swing to Gate

As we laid the foundations of Gate Petroleum Company, and the business began to come together, for me it was just the drop zone for exciting battles to come.

Most folks, when they get a taste of money, buy a boat, take time off, get a nice house, play golf and all that. It was just the opposite for me. The excitement of business took priority over all other activities.

It just so happened that I got into a business that suited my background. And when I got in there, and got a taste of money, it was Katy-bar-the-door. I liked what I was doing. I remember one time a major oil company representative came out there and offered me a job, and I said, "No, I'm doing fine." And I really was.

I'm one of the fortunate people who found their place in this world. And I did well; I loved it. I've always thought that in order to be happy you must love what you do for a living, and if you love it you will be successful. And if you are successful, you will be happy.

The Gate name was not an impulsive choice that I came up with overnight. I had planned to go into business. I kind of had it in the back of my mind that I would start my own station. And I also like Jacksonville very much, and it was known then as the "Gateway City." I wanted a one syllable name, easily pronounced, without any mystery about it, that could have an easily recognizable symbol. "Gate" fit all of these requirements. Another consideration was that a lot of Moncrief people couldn't read, and the Gate logo was easily recognized. Our slogan became "Swing to Gate."

After Moncrief, one of the earliest stations we built in Jacksonville was at Liberty and 21st Streets. It was a small corner, and we didn't have much expectation of the station, but a friend of mine owned the property and put up $12,000 for the building and leased it to me for $275 month. It turned out to be an excellent location and we made money from day one. So we got a few lucky breaks along the way.

When we started building more stations, I knew they must be spread out. I couldn't have them all in one market because price wars could break us. So immediately after the St. Augustine Road station, we started building stations outside of the Jacksonville market, in Orlando, Lakeland and Fort Myers.

Billy Weiss, whom I knew and worked with back at the old Billups Company, got in the oil business for himself in South Florida. He has been a friend of mine since I was a teenager, and the thing that really cemented our friendship was a station in Fort Meade, Florida. Gate had leased a piece of property down there back in the mid-1960s, and Billy had just bought a piece of property near ours. Fort Meade is a very small town. Billy was going to build a station there too, and it was obvious to both of us that there wasn't enough business for both of us. So we agreed Gate would build and run the station; Billy would put up half of the investment; and we would split the profits. Our friendship has continued all these years.

At times during Gate's first years, we had trouble making payroll, just like every other small company does. I can remember we always gave out the paychecks, but sometimes we'd ask some of our people, "Now, you hold yours till next Wednesday; you hold yours till next Tuesday"; and we knew some of them couldn't hold them at all. I kind of had a feel for who could hold on and who couldn't.

Back in the early 1960s, Gate was really having a hard time, and there was a situation here in Jacksonville where the retail price continually came down to cost on gasoline. The problem was an Eastern station on North Main Street which repeatedly would be the first to cut the price. Then a Sun station on Main Street, closer into town, would immediately meet it. That would start a price war in Jacksonville and the market would deteriorate in a matter of days, down to cost.

In the mid-1960s, I was traveling about 75,000 to 80,000 miles a year, in a Ford with the back seat out. We didn't have any trucks in the warehouse, and wherever I'd go, I'd carry several cases of oil with me in the back seat and trunk. That's how we'd deliver, and Billy Rhodes and I delivered most of the oil.

Although I was working hard and long hours and doing a lot of driving during those years, I loved it. We were growing fast, and making more money all the time. I think the test of whether someone likes what they are doing is if they look forward to Monday morning. And since Gate started I've looked forward to Monday morning because exciting things were happening.

Billy Rhodes and I decided the market was not as competitive or as volatile up in South Carolina. We started building stations in small South Carolina towns. We chose county seats, farming towns, and sometimes textile towns, usually with a population of around 15,000. We'd get the best piece of property in town, and we could still buy the property and build a station for about $50,000, sometimes up to $60,000.

Oliver William Collins, more commonly known as Uncle Bill, and I also traveled together, up to the Carolinas and Georgia and Virginia. Uncle Bill, who was not kin, claimed to be a farmer, run out of Mississippi by the boll weevil. He was a veteran of World War II, had been involved in real estate, and had worked for several oil companies. He was affectionately called by the Gate Brothers and by others who knew him, "the Old Sonofabitch." He was old as hell.

I had gotten to know the old gentleman during the Billups years. He was excellent in analyzing real estate, both locations and values. He and I must have traveled a million miles in a Ford during the 1960s and part of the 1970s. I carried a checkbook and if we saw a "for sale" sign, or even an unmarked property we thought would suit our needs, we'd pull over to the side of the road, find the owner, make him an offer, and sign the contract right there.

That gave us a tremendous advantage over the major oil companies, who attempt to buy options that sometimes take up to six months to get approved. I could write a binder right there and close within thirty days. We were able to buy property sometimes for cash, for a lot less money than it was worth, because we could act so quickly.

Uncle Bill, who has since died, was very helpful during those years. The Old Sonofabitch was also a philosopher and, as he said, a student of human nature. His observations on life in general were very astute.

Uncle Bill's theory on Watergate was that Nixon should not have been impeached, but should have been fired for being stupid because he didn't burn the tapes.

The Old Sonofabitch thought playing golf was a waste of time, and was designed for people who were too rich to work and too old to make love.

When the subject of Women's Liberation was brought up in Bill's presence, he stated his position clearly: "In the first place, women are not equal physically, emotionally, intellectually, or in any other damn way." Bill said the best way to handle women is to find out what they want to do and then make them do it.

One time Billy Rhodes, Uncle Bill, and I were traveling through South Carolina. It was necessary for me to phone one of Gate's competitors. From our car, parked close to the phone booth, Billy and Uncle Bill heard every word of my conversation, during which I was overly friendly and talked with great humility.

The phone conversation ended, I returned to the car, and we started down the highway. Uncle Bill, who had remained quiet up to this point, chided me from the back seat, "The Good Book says, 'He who humbles himself shall be exalted.'"

Uncle Bill and I had occasion to spend the night in Washington, D. C. I drove up to the check-in window at the big, new Marriott Motel, put down the driver's window, and asked the price of a room. Unbeknownst to either of us, the man at the check-in window had a two-way speaker system and could hear every word spoken in the car.

He informed me that the price for the room was fourteen dollars. Uncle Bill heard this on the speaker. Bill took his cigar out of his mouth and said, "Tell the thieving, yankee son-of-a-bitch that's too high."

The man very calmly replied, "Tell the old gentleman to come on and check in. I'm sure he will like it here. We even have inside plumbing."

One time in the late 1950s, Uncle Bill and I were traveling in Virginia. Every evening when we stopped for the day, Bill would burst out in a loud voice that could be heard over the entire hotel lobby, "Where is the whiskey store?" After this embarrassing incident occurred several times, I suggested to Bill that he stop this because we were new in this part of the country and we were trying to make a good impression.

The next evening, while we were checking into the plush General Washington Inn in Fredericksburg, Virginia, Bill stood proud and erect and remained quiet. During the elevator ride up to the room, Bill remained quiet. Down the hall into the room, Bill remained quiet. When we finally got into the room, he went immediately to the phone and smoothly made the following inquiry: "If a gentleman wanted to procure some 'Spirits of Fermenti', what would be the proper procedure?" After a few moments, he replied to the party on the other end of the line, "Thank you, Madame!" and hung up.

This country doesn't produce men like Uncle Bill anymore. He was the right man for the time. But those days are gone.

With Gate's negative float getting bigger we were making money and were able to expand from the Carolinas up to Virginia, then over to Kentucky. We were building not only a strong chain of service stations, but also a very able management team.

As we went along, we got more efficient and proficient in picking out locations. We knew what we were looking for and what worked for us and what didn't. Above all, we learned what not to do. Then we got more market acceptance, and we built better stations. Every station was built with the same basic design. They were profitable. We could have our after-tax money back on each new station in a matter of two, or certainly three, years. We were able to get away from the secondary locations on the back roads and move to the main streets.

We were making money, and Gate had a tremendous resource that it took several years to realize. The banks loved Gate Petroleum because we made tremendous cash deposits every night, which meant we had big balances. Once the bankers found out about the cash balances we had all over our system, they became very agreeable to loaning us large sums of money. That's the way we got the company expanded so fast. We dealt primarily with three banks: the Atlantic Bank, Barnett Bank, and the NCNB.

During those years, I was in the process of putting together the Gate Company and the Gate Brothers. Some of the people we hired had run stations for Billups Company, and some had not. We developed a tremendous camaraderie and all worked like hell and got along well together. The organization became known as "the Brothers."

The basic operations people at Gate were Billy Rhodes, who came in 1962, and later, Wayne Levitt, whom we got from another oil company. Marlene Giese and Louis Zemanek, who had worked for Billups, joined us not long after that and are still officers of the company. Other Billups employees who became Gate Brothers were Bobby Mathis, Robert Moody, Sammy Potts, Billy Jenkins, and Dizzy Locklear; Mac Matheny joined us to run the warehouse, which developed into a big business over the years. Theresa Clements joined us in 1975. With these Brothers I have a common unspoken bond, because our feet were wore off up to our knees while working for Billups.

Over the years, the ranks of the Gate Brothers grew to include Ray Day, Ron Kalapp, Don Davis, Ken Wilson, Steve Phillips, and Jim Citrano.

Louis Zemanek joined Gate about thirty years ago. Before he joined our ranks, he had no money, and no prospect of getting any. He worked hard and was well liked and had a very sunny disposition. Today, he is one of the main Brothers. However, Louie had one bad habit. He always wanted to borrow money. Seems like I couldn't walk down the hall without him asking me if the company could loan him some money. Finally, he asked me could he borrow $3,000; I've forgotten for what purpose.

I said, "Sure, Louie, we'll be glad to do that." So we cut him a check for $3,000 and gave it to him. When payday came, I presented Louie with his paycheck. The check was just like all his other paychecks, but in the money column it had $000.00. I explained to Louie that he would have to work for free until the money was repaid. That broke Louie from sucking eggs once and for all. He never again asked to borrow money from the company.

I took that check from Louie and had it framed, and it now hangs on my office wall. And the caption under the check says, "This man worked for free." Ever since then, when a Brother comes in and wants to borrow money, I simply point to the check, which explains the terms of such a loan, and gets them out of the notion.

I have a sign on the door of my office that says THINK BEFORE ENTERING. Sometimes when a Brother comes in with some wild scheme or idea that will not fly, I simply point to the sign on the door. The Brothers understand that means to go out, read the sign, come in again and start over.

Most of the Brothers didn't come from Billups. Several

of the Brothers came from firms we were doing business with. For instance, Jack Lueders, one of the main Brothers, was a CPA with our auditing firm. So was Ron Johnston. Neal McEachern came from Tenneco.

We have never had a Gate Brother come into the office and say, "I quit." We've had some that retired, and some died, and we have dismissed some for triflingism. And there's the old core of Brothers that are still with us, although they are much older now. When we started out, most of us were in our twenties and thirties. Over the years there have been around fifty Gate Brothers, but more than half of them are dead.

One of the things that I've gotten great satisfaction out of over the years, when I walk down the hall at Gate, is knowing that some of the Brothers are millionaires several times over. The unique thing about the Brothers was that when they came to Gate, all of them were short on money and long on ability. One reason they have done so well financially is the way the company is structured. The American free enterprise system does work, and when it is structured right, it is the best system for everyone.

Each one of those Brothers has his own division that he is in charge of, and he runs it. And I really do believe that we have assembled the best management people in Jacksonville to run these various assets. They are all extremely able, and they take great pride in Gate. And their morale and loyalty is strong.

When the company started to come together in the mid-1960s, we had a name, and a method of operating, and we had the strength of the Brothers which was more like a family than a company. We had the negative inventory, which also meant we had control at all times. In other words, we stuck our tanks every night and read our meters and we knew exactly where we were on the money. There was never much shortage; if there was any, we knew about it.

I know a man in Jacksonville that went in the hardware business about the same time Gate was being formed. He still runs that hardware store today, and it's a good one and he makes good money. But his ability to expand was extremely limited because the inventory was so big, and so complex, with the several thousand items he had to stock. In addition to that, he had to be there to run it.

In contrast, I could run a station in Hampton, South Carolina, from Jacksonville, and that would work because the man we put in Hampton was on commission. He had a good job, making between $1,000 and $2,000 a month. Back in those days, that was more than just about anybody else in that town was making, so he had a job that was worth protecting. He wouldn't do anything to jeopardize his job, so he would read the meters and put the money in the bank every night and take care of his business. He really felt like it was his own business, and to a certain extent it was; so we were able to run many service stations over a wide geographical area.

Once we had everything in place, the Gate Company grew just as fast as our finances would allow. During that period we had some tough times because of price wars. When the Hess Company came to Florida, all our stations were selling at or below cost, and we could last just so long. It seems we always got a break when we needed it and were able to come back. But there were some scary times, and times even after we got ten or twenty stations that we had trouble making payroll.

I think business today is a little bit over-sophisticated

and a lot of things are over-analyzed. American business today is still done on judgment and sixth grade arithmetic, and I think judgment, arithmetic, and gut feel are still better gauges of business than computer printouts are.

The Gate Brothers have always been hard workers. Laying up and burning daylight are still not permitted. If we have an advantage at Gate, it's that we get to work early and get a head start. That has become a kind of unwritten code of the Gate Brothers, and it does work.

Once an Atlanta banker was visiting down here. I took him to lunch at the River Club to impress him and talk about the possibility of a loan. He asked me who our lawyer was. I said, "Well, actually, we have two lawyers: One handles my business affairs and all my normal business legal work, and then I have a criminal attorney, and I use him on an as-needed basis." The banker became extremely nervous after that, and as a matter of fact he said there was an earlier flight back to Atlanta and he thought he would catch it. I never heard from him again.

My business lawyer is David Foster; he has also been my next door neighbor and is one of my closest friends. Dave is on the Board of Directors of the Gate Petroleum Company, and a stockholder. I remember back in 1960 I was using a lawyer from the Rogers, Towers, Bailey, Jones, and Gay firm. And I went to see Cecil Bailey, one of the partners, and I said, "Mr. Bailey, I want to get a young lawyer about my age, with a lot of ability, who I can depend on. I am not satisfied with my present arrangement with your law firm." He said, "Well, let me think about that for a few days."

In about four days he called me out at Moncrief and said, "I would like you to come to my office." I came in there one morning. Cecil Bailey had a plush office with the finest of decor, and antique furniture. He had with him a man who was about my age and had just gotten out of Harvard Law School.

His clothes were half wore-out. The front part of his tie was at least a foot longer than the back tail of his tie and hung down below his waist. His shoes gave no indication they had ever been polished. And his shoelaces came halfway up the holes provided for shoelaces, then were tied. Apparently they were broken and he had never bothered to get new ones. He wore white socks, the kind you buy at Woolworth's—six pair for ninety-eight cents. He wore an ill-fitting polyester sport coat that was frayed at the elbows. He was totally unimpressive.

Mr. Bailey said, "This is Dave Foster, and I think he is your man." I looked Dave up and down, and I can remember thinking very clearly, "This man will never do." I reluctantly agreed. I said, "Okay, that'll be fine," and Dave and I went down to the office to talk about legal matters. It took less than a week for me to be convinced that Mr. Bailey was right.

Dave is not only the best business lawyer, in my opinion, in the City of Jacksonville, his work goes much further than that. His analytical ability to look into different business situations is amazing. He has been involved in everything we have done for more than three decades. The contribution of his advice and counsel would be impossible to measure.

—Chapter Ten—

Walter G. Arnold, Criminal Attorney

T here came a time when I needed a lawyer fast. It was imperative that I had the best, because there was a possibility of jail. Cecil Bailey with Rogers, Towers said he hesitated to mention Walter Arnold because he was utterly ruthless, and I suggested that he pick up the phone and call him right away. And I went over and met Walter G. Arnold, Criminal Attorney.

Indeed, it was a fortunate day when I met Walter Arnold. For more than thirty years I have been his most loyal and consistent client. He and I have become very close friends. Over the past thirty years or so Walter and I have fought many battles together. We have fought the federal government, the state government, and assorted lawsuits.

Those bench-like chairs in his office were hard when I was thirty years old and they are even harder now. I have crouched in that wooden chair in front of his desk on many occasions when we felt surrounded, outnumbered, and our backs were to the wall.

On one occasion, Federal agents from Atlanta had us cornered. They were seeking jail and money. Things were so bad that Wayne Levitt, a Gate Brother, would not even be a witness for us. On more than one occasion, the State Attorney's office in Tallahassee was hot on our trail; they too were seeking jail and money. During these tough times, we always prevailed because of Walter's hard work, perseverance, patience with me, and the fact that when Walter goes into combat, "his reputation precedes him."

Walter is very tough and very smart, and when he is in

the courtroom, all eyes are on Mr. Arnold. He has tremendous presence and charisma. Being both tough and smart is a very good combination and is very rare. In addition, Walter looks mean. When he looks at you, he's actually got kind of a snarl on his face, and he has an intimidating personality.

After the Stockton, Whatley & Davin acquisition was closed, then came suing time. It seemed like everybody wanted to sue me. There was a series of lawsuits and threats of lawsuit. Walter sorted these out, and when all was said and done, they all got exactly what they deserved — zero.

I respect Walter Arnold more, probably, than any other citizen of Duval County. Walter is exactly twenty years my senior, and he is one of the most mentally tough people I have ever known. I think one of the reasons I respect him is because he reminds me of Pa in a lot of ways.

Mr. Arnold has very strong opinions on most matters of life. Still today, I go down to his home at Ponte Vedra before daylight on Saturday morning to drink coffee on my way to the gym, to get his views on political matters, economic conditions, and other issues of consequence. Walter Arnold told me long ago that Gate Petroleum Company was like a chain, and that I kept stretching and stretching it; and sooner or later the weakest link was going to break, and when it did, the whole thing would collapse.

One of our major battles began in the late 1970s, when the Justice Department decided the independent oil companies in the State of Florida were conspiring to fix gasoline prices. Now this on the surface sounded ridiculous, and I didn't even take it seriously, for the simple reason that we were selling gasoline for less than the major oil companies' prices. We were one or two cents less than the major oil companies all over the state, and always were. And yet they came after us instead of the major oil companies.

I remember one time I was in the office of another oil company, talking to them about some real estate. I asked them, "Have you ever had any trouble with the federal government on price fixing?" And they said, "No." I said, "How do you not have that trouble? They're on us all the time like a hawk on a June bug." One of them pointed down the hall and said, "We've got two floors of lawyers down there, and the government can come anytime they're ready."

I really believe one of the reasons they got on us was because they knew we did not have in-house legal staff. Anyway, they started poking around, and they would come in and ask a few questions, have a deposition or two and a grand jury hearing, and then they'd vanish for six months or so. We thought it was all over, and I didn't think it was serious anyway. They were slow as smoke, but they'd always come back. This went on for a couple of years.

Well, they were dead serious. Gate Petroleum Company was indicted along with eleven other independent oil companies in the state of Florida, for conspiracy to fix price. They gave me a subpoena that said, "United States of America against Herbert H. Peyton." I had my coaching session with Walter. I told him I was not against the United States, and I was going to straighten that out with the judge when I got down there. When I got to Tampa to appear before the Grand Jury, I asked to see the federal judge, and they took me to his office.

I remembered this federal judge; he had been a student at the University of Florida when I was there. Although I was not a friend of his, I remembered his name: Terrell Hodges. I got up there in his chambers and I told him in ordinary American talk that I was not against the United States of America, I was for them, and as a matter of fact, I had been in the Army.

He told me to get in that Grand Jury room and tell the truth, and if I didn't, he was going to put me in jail for perjury without a trial, and did I understand that? I went in the Grand Jury and stayed a couple of hours, and it was tough.

That afternoon I drove back to Jacksonville from Tampa. When I walked into my office, Darlene Cowan, my longtime secretary, told me that Walter had called three times, and as a matter of fact he was on the line now. Walter asked me how things went in Tampa, and I told him, "Fine." He then asked me how things went with the judge. I started telling him what I'd told the judge about me not being against the United States, and Walter said, "I know what you told him. I want to know what he told you." I said, "He told me 'get in there,' and he was going to 'put me in jail for perjury if I didn't tell the truth.'" Walter roared with laughter and hung up the phone.

I'm the only man in the State of Florida whose lawyer laughed when he'd been told by the judge he was going to put me in jail.

They later called Wayne Levitt, a Vice President of Gate Petroleum Company, to the Grand Jury. He went in there and stayed a couple of hours and they tried very hard to get him to say that Peyton told him to do this and that; Peyton told him to raise that price, call this fellow, and so forth and so on.

One time, before we went to the Grand Jury, I got a call from the Justice Department in Atlanta. They told me their lawyer was going to call my office about two o'clock, and they wanted to talk to my lawyer.

Although Walter was involved with this issue, I got Dave Foster to come to my office, and they did call promptly at two o'clock. Dave talked to them and it was not a conference call. When he concluded his call, and it came time to hang up, I was listening on an extension in Wayne's office. I thought well, the best way to do is to wait for them to hang up; then I would hang up. Dave hung up, and the attorney for the Justice Department didn't hang up. There I was, left with the receiver in my hand, and I could hear him breathing. I froze there for about two minutes.

I can remember putting my finger over very slowly and putting the receiver down. Wayne laughed. He said, "I'd give a thousand dollars, if he had come on the line and said, 'Peyton, we know you're there, and we're coming to get you!'" He thought it was very, very funny; he laughed and told all the Brothers.

About two months after that, Wayne was subpoenaed to appear before the Grand Jury. It was no longer funny. In fact, it was horrible. One afternoon I told Wayne to go home that night, get a good night's sleep, and wear his best suit in the morning. I wanted him to be at the office at six o'clock the next morning and go to town with me. We went downtown, and on the way he said, "Where are we going?" And I said, "Well, we're going to go down and visit Walter Arnold." Wayne sat quiet and still.

We got in Walter Arnold's office in the Gulf Life Tower, and we had Dave Foster in there with us. Walter sat at his desk, Dave sat in front of his desk, and I sat in the other chair in front of his desk. Wayne sat in back of us on the couch, quiet and still. During our meeting, Walter mentioned several times, "Wayne could testify to that." "Wayne would make a good witness," etc. Wayne remained quiet. This went on for about thirty minutes. Walter made these references several times, and once more, made the statement, "Well, Wayne will make a good witness."

All of a sudden, Wayne came unwelded and went into a rage, jumped to his feet and waved both arms and hollered that he wasn't going to be a good witness or a bad witness, he wasn't going to be a witness. He further stated that we should pay those people whatever they wanted, just pay them. I said, "Well, Wayne, that's fine, but you know we don't have much money." He said, "Just pay them and take it out of my pay. But just get rid of them."

Walter looked at me and said, "What's the matter with him?" And I said, "Walter, this man does not want to go to jail."

Well, we wound up pleading nolo contendere and paid the government $90,000. I never did believe that we did anything wrong, but nevertheless, we paid them off, because the trial would cost more than that, and we decided it was the best thing to do. Besides that, it seemed apparent Wayne was not going to be a good witness.

The truth about this whole ridiculous price fixing episode was that the bloodsuckers (major oil companies) were selling gasoline in every market in the state of Florida at higher prices than the cutthroats (independents), and yet during that period the federal government indicted no one in the state except the cutthroats. It is common knowledge in the oil business that the bloodsuckers hate the cutthroats like the devil hates holy water. Therefore, it has always been my feeling that the bloodsuckers are the ones that got the federal government on us.

— Chapter Eleven —

The Taste of Brass

When I reached my mid-thirties, Gate was established enough to allow me time for other interests. Translated, that means the wolf was away from the door. I had discovered over the years that I missed the excitement of the River Rat, the freight trains, and the paratroopers. I decided the time had come for more adventure.

I have always considered adventure to be gauged in three stages: the first stage is a quickening of the pulse rate; the second stage is butterflies in the stomach; and the third and most sought after is the taste of brass in the mouth, which is a direct result of the flow of adrenaline.

I developed a plan to put this excitement back into my life. In this regard I decided the challenge for me was in nature. I started a series of trips which over the next three decades included Canadian wilderness canoeing, whitewater canoeing in the Southeast, canoeing trips in Montana, ocean sailing up the coast, mountain climbing, and hiking through Linville Gorge in North Carolina.

To make these trips, it was necessary to be in top physical shape. I had a leg up on fitness because I've been running all my life. In the paratroopers we ran everywhere we went, and I have always done calisthenics. I tell people I've been in training for over forty years and I have stolen a decade.

I was running up and down Scott Mill Road in tennis shoes in the 1960s, before anybody in Jacksonville was running. I can remember when people would stop and ask if I wanted a ride home.

The running craze came to Jacksonville in the mid-seventies. The first River Run was in 1977, a 9.3 mile, fifteen kilometer run. I got my first Nike running shoes about a month before the race.

The race was in the first part of April, later in the year and a little later in the morning than when the River Run is held today, which meant it was hot as hell. I lined up and they blew the bugle and shot the gun and I was very hyped up and I ran as fast as I could go, which was considerably faster than my ability.

I ran over the Main Street Bridge and down Atlantic Boulevard and about six miles out, I was up there towards the front, and we started up the Hart Bridge, and half way up I fell down on the concrete. I thought somebody had hit me from behind, clipped me, as in football. What really happened was that the bear got me—I went down from exhaustion and heat stroke.

I got up and ran a few more steps and went down again — still didn't know what was happening. I got up and ran the third time, and I was unconscious before I hit the ground the final time. My chin hit the concrete. I woke up in a police car. It was scary, because I was in a police car and I looked over and saw the policeman and didn't know what had happened or where I was. He took me to an ambulance and they were hauling me to the Baptist Hospital. I talked them into taking me home instead, and that was a hard sell.

After that I got more interested in running. I trained better and talked to real runners about how to pace myself. I've run in all the road races in town, including the

River Run. The River Run has been going on for twenty years. I've run in all but four; twice I had broken bones and the other two times I had some other ailment. I've run in the Savannah and Jacksonville marathons, later, I started running in triathlons. I compete in the ocean marathon swims every summer. It has taken a long time, but I have finally figured out that I do not enjoy playing games, all I like to do is race—any kind of race.

In the triathlon, you swim, bike, and run. I really got pretty good at that; as a matter of fact, for awhile I could beat any son-of-a-bitch in Jacksonville over fifty years old on a good day. But the way I've been able to win is through attrition; there are not many of us out there at my age.

I work out eight to ten hours a week, and my exercise routine consists of running, Nautilus, free weights, swimming, and biking. Some Sunday mornings I bike down J. Turner Butler Boulevard from Mandarin to Ponte Vedra, have breakfast at the Inn, and ride back home, which is a fifty mile round trip. I usually run three or four times a week.

A lot of people exercise to control weight or because they feel they should, but I truly enjoy it. It is kind of like a hobby for me. My weight has been the same since I graduated from high school. My pulse rate is below fifty, which means I'm subject to falling asleep in a meeting, especially in the afternoon, and do on occasion.

The problem for the last twenty years, when tripping time came, has been finding somebody to go with me. The Brothers instinctively knew very early that they did not want to go on these trips with me. I would suggest a canoe trip or a sail in the ocean, or mountain climbing, or a hiking trip through Linville Gorge, and they would say no, they wouldn't be able to go, they had other plans. But there was one person I could rely on to go, and he would go anywhere. That was Mitchell Rhodes, Billy Rhodes' son.

Mitchell is a longtime Gate Brother, and when he was in his teens and early twenties, he would go with me on these trips. He was the only volunteer. We had several canoe trips in the Carolinas, hiking trips, and that rough sail up the coast from Mandarin to Charleston, South Carolina that had so terrified by Mother as she kept vigil From North Carolina.

Mitchell and I went in my 25-foot Morgan, the River Rat II. His mother gave some resistance to this. I remember when he told his mother that he and I were going to sail to Charleston, his mother told him, "Herby is a hell of a man, and you are a hell of a fool."

When Mitchell and I sailed up the St. Johns River, tornado watches were up. We sailed up the coast in the midst of a massive storm that covered the entire Southeast. The waves were twelve to fifteen feet and the wind gusts must have been fifty miles per hour. The jib was all we needed because the wind was coming out of the south. I can remember sitting back in the stern of the boat with the tiller, and looking around, and following us would be a wall of water fifteen feet tall. We hunkered down thinking it was coming in the boat, but the boat was well constructed, and it would rock and roll and somehow ride the crest of the waves. Although we took in a lot of water, we never did get completely flooded.

We both stayed scared to death and half seasick the whole time, and ate very little. We took two hour watches. We had left my dock in Mandarin at daylight one morning, cleared the St. Johns River jetties in early afternoon, and started up the coast, staying ten to twenty miles offshore. We could see land some of the time, and some of the time we couldn't. We sailed all night, and that was one of the scariest nights of my life. It was black as Egypt and the River Rat II was heaving and dipping, and I thought any minute the mast was going to break off, but we made good time and scooted right up the coast.

We passed Savannah at daylight the next morning and got into Charleston at twilight that night, having sailed for two days and one night. I was very delighted to pull up to the Charleston marina. I don't think I've ever welcomed sitting on dry land as much. Mitchell held up very well during this trip. I remember at one point the jib got away and it popped like a shotgun when the line broke. Mitchell came and sat down beside me, white as a sheet, and he said, "What do you want me to do now?" He thought the end was near.

Mitchell had a very positive attitude back in those days, and when I said, "Let's trip," he'd agree to go anywhere. Mitchell was always agreeable to go because it was his only way to get off work.

When Mitchell was in his early twenties I took him to the Appalachian Mountains of North Carolina to hike through Linville Gorge, the roughest terrain east of the Mississippi River. It has 800-foot rock cliffs on each side and the Linville River rushes through it. You enter in the headwaters and walk and climb for two or three days until it comes out about twenty miles later into Lake James near Morganton, North Carolina.

The house my father built near Linville has always been a family retreat. Twelve miles away is Wiseman's View, overlooking the Gorge. The Gorge is beautiful all year, but it is particularly beautiful in the fall, when the leaves are turning.

Linville Gorge, is to me, the last retreat of Nature. From Wiseman's View, the message from the Gorge is very clear to me. The river roaring deep in the Gorge says loudly, each time I go, that civilization has pushed nature all over this continent in the last century, it has built highways and bridges and telephone lines, it has dumped sewage and polluted, it has cleared and cultivated and caused erosion, but this is one place where nature has made its stand.

The roar of that river, coming out from the bottom of that gorge, seems to defy civilization. It seems to say: "You sonofabitches think you've won, but you'll never take this place, and I defy you to come down here! We will do battle on my terms and on my land, and I'll make you regret that you ever saw or heard of The Gorge."

Linville Gorge is exactly like it was a thousand years ago. There are no trails, there are no beer cans, there are no telephone poles or roads, there are no bridges. There is no access to the Gorge. There are no houses and there never will be. This area, in Pisgah National Forest, is exactly like it always has been.

When you enter Linville Gorge, you realize immediately that the gorge is very serious, and it resents you being there. When you get through the Gorge, if you do, you don't have the feeling you have whipped the Gorge—you have the feeling that the Gorge has tolerated you for a couple of days, and you're damn lucky to get out of there alive. The whole thing is a trap that has been planned for a thousand years. Mother Nature is there, enticing you and seducing you: "Come on in, it's nice and beautiful down here."

When I go to the Gorge I view it as combat, and the

enemy is Mother Nature. She will fight you every inch and mile of the way, and she will send you retreating to civilization, completely whipped, physically, emotionally and mentally, and she will dare you to come, to set foot in the Gorge again.

The unbelievable thing about the Gorge is that it has never been penetrated. There has never been any timber cut in the Gorge, because nobody could get it out of there; there has never been a road, because nobody could build a road up the cliff. It is completely isolated and it has never been raped or assaulted by man and it never will be.

Inside the Gorge, the roar of the river is relentless, like standing by waterfalls all of the time. After awhile, the noise wears you out. You can't talk much to whomever you are with, and the noise exhausts you and defeats you mentally if you let it.

You make your way down one side of the river or the other, then run into a cliff or a rock bigger than a house blocking your side of the river, and you have to double back. So although it is twenty miles long as the crow flies, you're retracing your path and climbing sheer cliffs, and it is so frustrating and feels so futile when you have struggled across the river and gone a quarter of a mile or even a half mile and run into another boulder and have to double back again and start over.

There are so many different challenges in the Gorge and you develop a special kind of claustrophobia. It is like being in a maze. Nature has gone wild.

When you get into situations like that created by human beings, you say, well they wouldn't close it all off, they'd give you a way out, it's just a puzzle you've got to figure out. But Mother Nature doesn't give you any options. There is no puzzle. You can sit there on a rock and look for twenty minutes. No one has written a guidebook. You have got to figure out how to do it, and you have got to be damn careful, because you cannot afford to get injured. Brother Bear is there, and Slim the Snake, and you have got to be constantly on the watchout for them.

Mitchell, being a flatlander from Florida, was unaccustomed to the mountains. My trip with Mitchell was an extremely rough trip and he balked like a Georgia mule. He refused to go forward, and backtracked his way out of the Gorge. Being down there, closed in with the relentless noise, got to Mitchell and he came apart like a two-dollar watch.

As a matter of fact, his father told me that Mitchell was in such a mental state when he returned that he wouldn't even climb a ladder in the service station to hang up a banner because he didn't want to get his feet off the ground. That was Mitchell's last trip with me, and my efforts to enlist other Brothers have failed. I have been back to the Gorge, but without Mitchell.

At one point on the trip through the Gorge after I had escorted Mitchell out and had returned to the Gorge by myself, when I was extremely tired, I had to cross the river because cliffs made the left side impassable. I walked out on a log to get part way across; then I was going to step in the river, which I assumed was shallow, and walk the rest of the way across. I made two mistakes: number one, the river was not shallow, it was over my head; number two, the current was very swift and I stepped off the log on the upcurrent side, which meant the current immediately washed me over the log.

I was caught over the log, pinned at the waist, with my

feet under the log, and my shoulders over the top of the log. The backpack on my back was catching the current and holding my head under water. I was unable to breathe. I came very close to losing consciousness. The only thing that kept me from drowning was that my pack's waist strap broke, and the current then forced my pack off over my head; and when it did, I was able to lift my head out of the water and eventually get off the log.

I swam over to the other shore and threw up all the water I had inhaled, then went downstream about a quarter of a mile to recover the pack, washed up on a rock. The scary thing about it was I was down there by myself. There was nobody to help me, and if that pack had not come off, I would have drowned in less than a minute.

I learned when you step off a log into water, you can't assume how deep it is. You can't ever step off upstream because the water will knock you back into the log and hold you. If I had stepped off on the downstream side, even though it was over my head, I would have been all right. But when that happened I had been up there for two days and I was exhausted and not thinking very clearly.

I have had an ongoing battle with the Gorge for many years and I'm not through yet. I have attacked the Gorge several times and each time was a near disaster and I came out crawling and exhausted. I have heard black bears growling in the Gorge. One time I almost stepped on a rattlesnake.

Once, before our fateful Gorge trip, Mitchell and I were on a canoe trip in South Carolina, and at midafternoon came to a dam. We asked the damkeeper if he was going to release any water that night, and he said, "No." We went down the river, about five miles from the dam, and set up camp for the night on a sandbar. Mitchell woke me up about eleven o'clock that night and said, "The water is rising." I said, "No, no, hell no. Go back to sleep."

I know well the sounds of water. I know what a whirlpool on the Mississippi River sounds like, and the laughing sound that water makes in the rapids, and the roar that the Linville River makes in the Gorge. I also am familiar with the gurgling, rustling sound of rising water as it pushes through the dead grass and sticks on the banks. As I lay there, I did hear that rustling sound.

I got up and the water was lapping up on the sandbar. The damkeeper had opened the dam full force. We were able to evacuate to the high bank just before it overtook the camp. The canoe, which was tied to a log on the sandbar, was out in the middle of the river. I had to swim out there in the middle of the night to get it. We went on down the river and got up on a high bank and slept the rest of the night.

On another trip, Mitchell and I had to cross a swamp, about sixty miles wide, in a canoe. We ran out of food, and the only thing left was some apple juice. I drank apple juice until I can't stand the sight of it even today. We were paddling the canoe and I got out on a sandbar, and I remember I couldn't even stand up straight or walk, I was so exhausted.

About the time the River Run began in Jacksonville, I became interested in mountain climbing, and my climbing partner and mentor was Ted Kilpatrick. He and I went on several trips. We went out to Mount Ranier near Seattle, Washington, for mountain climbing school. We attempted to climb Mount Ranier on two occasions, and we attempted to climb the Grand Tetons in Wyoming one January. I had planned my biggest mountain climbing trip, a really big league trip, on Mount McKinley for the summer of 1983. McKinley is the tallest and toughest mountain in North America, and also happens to be the northernmost major mountain in the world.

I trained for this trip for about a year, and got all the necessary equipment, which cost close to $2,000. We got airline tickets, hired a guide, and were due to leave on a Friday. On the Tuesday before that Friday, I got a phone call from New York, saying that we were high bidder on the Stockton, Whatley & Davin real estate. That trip was canceled and I have never been able to get away for another climb. With mountain climbing, you can't say, "Well, I'll leave on Tuesday and come back on Friday." You are never sure when you will get back. It depends on the mountain and the weather.

The unique thing about my mountain climbing experiences was that I never made a summit; something always happened. On the first trip to Ranier, two people in the party in front of us were caught without adequate shelter in a whiteout (a storm that moved in suddenly), and froze to death. We were not able to proceed; we were about 2,000 feet from the summit and they evacuated everybody off the mountain.

On my second trip to Ranier, we were about 1,000 feet from the summit and a rock about the size of a basketball came tumbling down the mountain and hit our guide in the thigh, breaking his leg, and we had to pissant him off the mountain.

Also on our second trip to Ranier, before the guide's accident, we were on a real steep incline, on a rope team, and I lost my footing and started tumbling down the mountain. When you fall and start sliding, you're supposed to go into an ice axe arrest immediately to stop your slide. I got out of control and because of my slow reflexes I didn't get the message quick enough. Ted Kilpatrick was ahead of me on the rope team and he immediately went into an ice axe arrest position and the rope caught me right before I went into a crevasse several hundred feet deep. If it hadn't been for his quick thinking, I would have pulled us all into the crevasse.

When we went to the Tetons in Jackson Hole, Wyoming, in the middle of January, it was fourteen below zero when we got off the plane, and thirty-five below at night, with several feet of snow. Our guide met us and the night before our departure from Jackson Hole, we went to an old log cabin steak house. I went up to the fire and was warming myself while we waited for the food, and started talking with some oldtimers who were sitting around the fire in rocking chairs. I said, "Well, we are from Florida, and we are going to climb the Tetons, starting in the morning." They were quite distressed, because nobody out there climbs the Tetons in wintertime, and they became quite interested in our climb.

The next morning we lit out; we had a party of six. By the first night, one of those had hypothermia and could have very easily died, but didn't. Our guide worked on him most of the night to get his circulation back up. Two of the party evacuated off the mountain the next morning, retreating to the motel.

Four of us kept going up the mountain. That afternoon we got into a wind, and with the temperature at about twenty-five below zero, the chill factor made it about seventy below zero. The wind blew right through us. We walked up the mountain on old Army skis, with treads on the bottom so you didn't slide while walking. Each of us had about an eighty pound pack on our back.

It is unbelievable the amount of hurt you endure while trying to go up a mountain, with much ice and snow on a steep incline with a full field pack, in very thin oxygen. Those three factors combine for an unimaginable amount of strain and pain. You are convinced, many times during the day, that you cannot make another step, and that your body will refuse to go, refuse to move, but you somehow struggle along.

One of my skis malfunctioned and I had to take off my gloves to fix it. Although it took less than three minutes, I got frostbite on three fingers of my right hand. That night we finally made it into a cave out of the wind, and had a pretty good night's sleep. The next morning, we started out again, and by this time we were at about 12,000 feet.

By this time I was delirious and just barely coherent. The guide was concerned about me. He came back to the rear where I was stumbling and asked me if I was alright.

I told him in short order to worry about his own self, that I was doing fine; I had been in training since before he was born, and furthermore, I was just getting warmed up. We proceeded up the mountain about another hour; he came back again and I was delirious and got even more belligerent; and they decided to turn back. It was a good thing, because I was barely on my feet by that time. Once again, we failed to make a summit. I later found out that high altitude frequently has this affect on people.

Mountain climbing is the absolute ultimate sport, truly a life and death struggle between you and nature, and the most challenging and demanding sport I've ever been involved in. It requires total dedication. For production of adrenaline, it compares favorably with jumping out of an airplane. You cannot halfway do mountain climbing. You're out there and it's you against the mountain, it is all out war.

Ted Kilpatrick has continued to climb mountains and has since climbed some major peaks. Someday I plan to do more climbing, even though I seem to be snakebit when it comes to making a summit.

In the same period with the mountain climbing, I ran across another trip-taker, Randy Hardee, who lives in Jacksonville. Randy was chosen because he is six-feet-three and weighs 260 pounds, and his function was if anything happened in the woods, he could put me over his shoulder and pissant me out. If anything happened to him, it was every man for himself. Because of his tremendous bulk, he went by the appropriate name of Biggie.

Biggie and I decided the thing for us to do was to go to northern Canada and make a hundred-mile canoe trip down the rapids of a remote river up near the Arctic Circle, with no civilization, no roads, no access, until you wind up in an Indian village. We set out for the Albany River in northern Ontario, which runs into Hudson Bay.

We flew commercial airlines to Thunder Bay, Canada, and after a big meal, spent the first night in a motel. There was one problem the next morning when we left the motel to drive north in our rented car. I took the tent to prop the door open while we loaded equipment back and forth, and unbeknownst to us—it was still well before daylight and black as Egypt—the tent was left propping the door open. We didn't realize this until much later.

We drove 500 miles north on dirt roads and arrived at this camp, expecting them to run out and say, "Glad to see you. I've never been to Florida. I bet it's beautiful down there," and so forth. They hardly looked up when we came in. They said, "Oh, yeah, I heard you were coming." Then there was great delay because it was too foggy to fly the plane, and because the water level was low.

Of course, by this time Biggie and I were pretty hyped up, ready to get out, and we kept asking Ernie, the pilot, when we were going to take off. We were outside this little cabin, within earshot of Ernie, and one of these old time Canadians came in there and said, "Who are those fellows out there?" And he said, "Those sonofabitches are from Florida and they don't know where in the hell they are going, and I've told them three times we couldn't take off in this fog."

Towards the middle of the day, the sun did bust through and the fog lifted, and we strapped the canoe, which we had rented from Ernie, to the pontoons, loaded up our equipment and took off. The plane was at least twenty-five years old, and it looked like a Model A Ford. I don't know how in the hell it ever got off the lake. When we took off it lurched, shimmied and shook and I thought it never would get airborne, but it finally did and we got up to 500 feet, which is about 400 feet above those pine trees, and we were flying due north and passing over lakes, and I was just getting settled in the back seat.

The engine was worn out, and all of a sudden it stopped. It stayed off I guess for about thirty seconds and we started down—it seemed like thirty minutes. Biggie turned around and looked at me and he was white as a sheet. We couldn't have lasted but a few more seconds before we hit those pine trees, but the engine sputtered and started again. Ernie told us later that the engine had cut off because of condensation in the gasoline.

Ernie took us up to this river and let us out on a sandbar, and he took off waving goodbye, and we were delighted. It was nice weather, late afternoon, and we had all our equipment, and were getting ready to go on a great adventurous trip. We had a real small map that didn't give any detail, but we knew exactly where we were going and we knew there were many rapids between us and our destination. We had no idea how remote it was, how wild it was, and that we would not see a human being for almost a week, or any sign of civilization.

So we got out on the sandbar. Biggie said, "I'm gonna go out and look around a little bit, while you set up camp." And I said, "Fine." Biggie came back in about twenty minutes and said, "I've got some bad news." I said, "What is it?" He said, "I saw a bear track out there bigger than your head." And I said, "Well, I've got some bad news, too, Biggie." He said, "What is it?" I said, "We haven't got any tent. We left it back in Thunder Bay."

So there we were, a thousand miles from nowhere, no tent, in northern Canada near the Arctic Circle in September, which meant cold nights: about fifty degrees in the daytime, down in the mid-thirties at night. We rigged up the canoe on the sandbar, so that we slept with our heads up under the canoe and our feet extended out at right angles from the canoe.

I got up the next morning at daylight. We always had to put the food away from our camp and up in a tree so as not to attract the bears, and we had that all rigged up. I started to make a fire and asked Biggie how he slept and he said he hadn't slept at all. I said, "What do you mean?" He said, "I was watching for Brother Bear and Slim the Snake."

Anyway, we took off in our canoe. We would come

around a bend in the river and listen. If we heard rapids, we would pull over to the shore and scout ahead to see how bad they were and whether we could go through them or not. A lot of times they were so rough we couldn't get a canoe through them and had to portage.

One time we did that and decided we would have to cross to the other side of the river to portage, because there were horrible rapids below. We were crossing the river, and that was fine, except we got too close to the rapids, got caught in the current, and started down. Biggie hollered, "Hit it, Red!" and we paddled as hard as we have ever paddled in our lives, and I do believe the canoe came up out of the water; but we did manage to make it to the other side.

When we were portaging we had to be careful to keep a gun near at all times in case a grizzly bear came out of the woods. About the third day out, we were both already weary when a late afternoon storm moved in. Now we had a very real danger up there of getting hypothermia, because we had no tent, and we had to be careful about getting wet, especially in the afternoon or at night. In the middle of the day when the sun was out, it would be alright. This particular afternoon a storm moved in, and the wind was blowing thirty or forty miles an hour, and the rain was coming down so hard it felt like chips of wood hitting us.

We started looking for a place to camp. We really wanted to get in a cave or somewhere out of the weather. This was fine except on each side of the river, were high banks, and in the rain and wind we couldn't pull that canoe up the bank. We didn't know what was at the top of the bank, either—whether it would be suitable for camping or not. We kept going a little further and a little further down the river, looking for a place to get out, where we could get up on a sandbar or a short bank.

Twilight came, and we became desperate. We were running out of time. Along about this time Biggie looked across the river and saw this big tree that had recently blown over, roots and all. So at his suggestion, we paddled over. We got in the hole where the root ball had been, and pulled the canoe over the top of the hole and spread our sleeping bags down in the hole. We were dry and snug as a bug in a rug. Biggie had unbeknownst to me brought a little bottle of bourbon with him. We both had a shot of liquor and went to sleep and had a fine night's sleep. Then and there, I decided Biggie had much savvy in the woods, and he has been at the top of the trip-taking list ever since.

We proceeded down the river for several more days, still not seeing any sign of humans, not even an airplane going over. We were getting low on food and getting weaker every day. I think we were on the river six days and we always thought we knew where we were, relative to the Indian village, but we were never quite sure. We came around the bend, and there was a dock and a group of Indian shacks on the left bank. I have never seen a more welcome sight.

We paddled over to the dock as fast as we could. There were two Indians on the dock, working on an outboard motor, and we pulled up and said, "Howdy! How are ya'll today?" They just looked up and grunted, "Ugh." Didn't even speak. We got out, pulled the canoe up on the dock, and found out there was a Hudson Bay store nearby. We went in and there was an Englishman running that store. He took good care of us and invited us up to his apartment above the store that night, and we had a steak dinner. It was much needed.

We got on the two-way radio the next morning and radioed Ernie to come get us. That Indian village was the most dismal place I have ever been. It was unbelievable. About a hundred Indians lived there, all on welfare, supported by the Canadian government. The Indians didn't work; there wasn't any work for them to do up there. They would hunt and trap a little bit in the winter. But they would take lumber the government had flown up there so the Indians could build homes, and chop it up for firewood. That's how trifling they were.

That is the godawfullest country. And those Indians, they are something. The Indians expressed no interest and no emotion about us being in their village. We were just there. We tried to be friendly with them, but most of them spoke in the unknown tongue. They looked at us and that was the extent of their communication. And you would think that they would be curious, because no one ever comes there. But they didn't give a damn about that.

I can remember waiting for that plane the next day, and we weren't sure Ernie was going to come and get us. Ernie had not been overly friendly with us. There wasn't any way out of there, except on that airplane. There were no roads within several hundred miles. It was a gray, dismal, morning, and there was a graveyard up there about one hundred years old and full of weeds, and I told Biggie if anything happened to me, for God's sake, don't bury me up here, take me back to Florida. We were delighted to see Ernie's plane on the horizon.

We strapped the canoe on Ernie's plane and he flew us back to the camp, and we got in our car and drove south, and flew back home. Biggie had really proved his worth to me. Biggie was a good man in the woods.

Biggie has one other trait that is very desirable. Even today, about once a week in the summer, he meets me at six o'clock in the morning at the Ponte Vedra gym and we swim out beyond the breakers and then north for one mile. I take Biggie along for shark protection purposes. It is very hard to get volunteers to swim in the ocean at earliest dawn. As a matter of fact, we've been doing this for several years and have yet to see another swimmer.

Chapter Twelve

A New Hustle

The first energy crisis hit in 1973. Several things happened to Gate during the energy crisis. One was that we didn't have enough gasoline to run our stations during normal hours. Another effect of the energy crisis was that we couldn't build service stations anymore, because we couldn't get gasoline. But every gallon we had, we sold at the top legal price, and we made a lot of money and had an accumulation of profits. We had to invest that money in a business, or pay an accumulated surplus income tax, or declare a dividend. It was time to get a new hustle, so Gate went into its first diversification: a potato farm in Hastings, Florida.

We bought a 500-acre potato farm, and Mitchell Rhodes, Billy Rhodes' son, ran it. He had been supervising service stations for us up in Atlanta. He didn't know a thing about farming, and he went down there and went to work and learned the business, and became one of the most respected farmers in the Hastings area.

The potato farm did well. In some years, we made big money. Our success in Hastings was due to Mitchell's perseverance. He worked hard, and he stayed with it, and it was tough as hell sometimes.

I was on the Board of Directors of the Barnett Bank of Jacksonville then, and about that same time, developers around the country and in Jacksonville were having a hard time. The interest rates were high and the country was kind of in a recession. I'd sit on that board and hear all those stories and everybody's problems, but Gate was doing fine.

We had to deal with all kinds of regulations from the Energy Department and a lot of red tape and a lot of bother, but we got through it the best way we could. The thing that made it all worthwhile was we were making money. We had just started buying from Phillips Petroleum Company in 1972 and we didn't have a contract with them. We were concerned that they might cut us off.

We had a friend at Phillips who told us we should be very careful with the company and not complain about anything, because they could shut us off, and no matter what they did, not to complain. Historically, when a supplier called to tell you they were going up a quarter cent, you just automatically cussed him out and told him what a no good sonofabitch he was.

Sure enough, Phillips Petroleum called me one Friday afternoon and said, "We've got bad news for you. We're going up on your product three cents a gallon on all grades." Well, at that time, that was the biggest price increase that had ever happened in the history of the industry. Price increases prior to that had been handled in increments of one-half cent or one-quarter cent.

And I said, "Well, that will be fine. Anything else?" The energy crisis worked itself out, and we came out of it very strong financially, and started expanding at an even faster rate.

As part of our diversification, in 1976, we built Bigtree Racquet Club in Mandarin. We later sold it.

Right after the energy crisis, we bought a group of twenty-two Sun Oil Company stations. Sun was pulling out of the state of Florida. We $1.7 million, and we took those properties and built Gate stations on the best ones. Some we leased and a lot of them we sold.

I remember one particular Sun property we bought, in Ocala, Florida, on U. S. 301. In a matter of months, we sold it to Midas Muffler for about five times what we'd paid for it. We got out of that Sun deal some of the best stations in the company today. We later bought five more Sun stations, and they worked out very well, too.

In 1978, Fitzhugh Powell, a long time friend of the company who had sold me my first business insurance policy for Moncrief back in 1960, came to see me. He told me there was someone coming to town he wanted me to meet—Joe Luke. Joe worked for Masonite in Meridian, Mississippi, and he had figured out there was more asphalt felt consumed in Florida than there was produced, and there was a market here. He had all this in a book he had put together. It was all statistics and cost of building a plant and margins, etc. And I read the book and I couldn't get the Brothers interested in it; they wouldn't even read the book.

On Joe's second visit, he impressed me because of his straight talk, and I said, "Joe, how much are you worth working?" And he said, "$35 thousand a year." And I said, "Well, how much money have you got?" And he said, "None." And I said, "Well, the trouble with this plant, as I see it, is if we build a plant and it doesn't work out, you'll go back to Mississippi, and I don't want a roofing plant." And he said, "I don't want to go back to Mississippi." And on that basis, we formed a company, Gate Roofing Company.

Joe went to Green Cove Springs and built a roofing plant. His book was wrong; it turned out much better than he had anticipated. We started making money the second month down there. We expanded it, doubled the capacity; it is now the largest asphalt felt plant under one roof in the

United States; it runs twenty-four hours a day. Joe brought the plant manager, Bill Saunders, and his salesman, Pete Vining, with him. Bill later died of cancer. Pete stayed with us after we sold the roofing plant.

The big thing we got out of Gate Roofing was not the roofing plant, but Joe Luke. Joe turned out to be one of the best executives in Jacksonville. We found out in years to come if we bought a business, he could go in the first day and run it and get control of it, although he knew very little about the business.

In 1980, Bryant Skinner Company and Gate Petroleum Company went into a joint venture for the development of the Southpoint office park, which eventually developed into a 250-acre plush complex. Its success was attributable to a very unique circumstance in Jacksonville at that time. Construction of J. Turner Butler Boulevard opened up a new corridor to the beaches, and Southpoint was in the northeast quadrant of I-95 and J. Turner Butler Boulevard. The Southpoint site was close to downtown Jacksonville, yet had remained undeveloped; therefore, when the new boulevard opened, Southpoint turned out to be some of the best commercial real estate in the Jacksonville area.

The basic mission of Southpoint was buying land by the acre, putting in the infrastructure, and selling it by the square foot. Bryant Skinner was well qualified for this job, as he had done it well for most of his adult life. He was a good teacher and I learned a lot about commercial real estate from him.

The unique circumstances of the J. Turner Butler corridor provided another opportunity for Gate. I took the lessons I had learned from working with Bryant Skinner on Southpoint and used them to establish Deerwood Park.

As a result of the SWD acquisition, Gate was able to develop Deerwood Park, a business office park located on the northeast and southeast corners of the intersection of Southside Boulevard and J. Turner Butler Boulevard. For several years it had been a big sand pit. But now it is one of the most prestigious office parks in Northeast Florida with buildings full of people from major corporations such as AETNA, Barnett Bank, Merrill Lynch, BellSouth, Blue Cross & Blue Shield of Florida, IBM, Lamborghini, Superstock and Vistakon. This division, which is run by Joe Luke and Ken Wilson, is very successful.

Gate is privately owned, and the disadvantage of that system is that we don't have any way to generate money other than earnings or borrowing from banks. The first thing you have to do is give the government almost half your earnings. The second thing is that you can't make enough money to expand and take advantage of the opportunities that are out there, and as a result of that you're constantly trying to borrow money from the bank because there's no other source.

Gate is unique in our structure in that we don't have any outside stockholders. Every stockholder is an employee of Gate. There are about sixty stockholders of Gate, including myself. And the same is true of the board—the board of Gate Petroleum Company is made up of the officers of Gate Petroleum Company. And therefore our goals or our interests are the same—we don't have stockholders pulling in one direction and management in another direction and board in another direction. This system has some obvious disadvantages, in that we lack checks and balances, but the big advantage is that Gate can move fast.

Now, our approach to diversification developed in a particular pattern, which we have followed for many years. We buy assets, or groups of assets, for cash. Then we sell off what we don't want to operate, and we keep the operations that are best for us. We also keep the best personnel. Most of our diversifications have turned out better than we anticipated.

I think this is true for two reasons. One is that very few people are willing to pay cash when you get up over ten million dollars. The second reason is that a lot of these companies we bought would be very hard for a publicly owned company to buy, because the publicly owned company is interested in what their earnings are next quarter or next year. Gate management was concerned with that, too, but we were more concerned with the long-term value and earning capacity of these assets.

The large cash acquisitions are usually too large for a private company to buy, and many times they are not designed for a publicly owned company either, because in many cases such acquisitions don't have any immediate impact on earnings. Our Blount Island acquisition is a prime example of that.

I've found in these cases, that when somebody wants to sell something, and you can make a cash offer with a fast closing, it's always worth a test to find out how badly they want out.

The reason Gate works is that we have a lot of discussions about what to do, but when all that's over, I say, "That's fine, and here is what we are going to do." In most companies, the process is more complicated than that. I am not always right, but under our system we don't get gridlocked and paralyzed because of indecision.

On most of our acquisitions, I have gotten very little encouragement from the Brothers. In fact, when we bought Blount Island, most of the Brothers were against it, and there was much emotion and hell-raising about it.

You can't have a seminar about every thing that comes down the pike. You would never reach any decisions, never take any actions. That is the reason that Gate has been able to do things that other companies couldn't do. Most publicly owned companies would not do the things Gate has done, such as getting leveraged and taking chances and buying a company bigger than they were.

In 1980, Fitzhugh Powell came into my office and said there was a company we ought to buy in Jacksonville: the construction division of Houdaille-Duval.

Houdaille-Duval was primarily in the manufacturing business. They produced automobile parts, and they had a big construction company in Florida and had decided to get out of the construction business and were in the process of liquidating. They had five asphalt plants and several prestressed concrete plants. I went over to see Bill Burns, the president, on Riverside Avenue, and we had a very good conversation.

He agreed to sell us the five asphalt plants and the Jacksonville prestressed concrete plant, and the price was about $10 million cash. Barnett Bank loaned us the money and we closed in about thirty days.

We operated the asphalt plants for about a year and sold them to two buyers, a South Florida company and a Virginia company. We wound up making several million dollars on the asphalt plants. We still have the prestressed concrete plant on Heckscher Drive in Jacksonville. In addition to prestressed concrete, it manufactures Gate-core, a hollow-core concrete slab used in multistory construction. The plant is run by Benny Cleghorn, and his assistant Henry Davis, who were both with Houdaille-Duval. We have expanded the size and modernized the plant, and it does tremendous business; it is one of the best in the South.

About a year after we bought Houdaille-Duval, Bill Burns called me and said they wanted to sell one remaining asset, a prestressed hollow-core concrete plant in Houston, Texas. He asked if we had any interest in it. I took a couple of Brothers and went out there and looked at it. Physically, it was better than the Jacksonville plant in some regards. It was worth about $2 million.

So we had a meeting in my office with about twelve of the Brothers. I told them we had been out to Houston to look at the concrete plant. I said, "I think we ought to offer them a million dollars for it; it's worth a lot more." I remember during the discussion, Billy Rhodes said, "We not only don't have the million dollars to buy the concrete plant, we don't have the price of a plane ticket to go out and look at it."

It was that kind of thinking that was to cause the first vote to be negative. I might also add that he was exactly right. And although the purchase price was a million dollars, it would cost us almost another million in working capital, so we were talking $2 million.

When voting time came we went around the room counterclockwise, and the first four Brothers voted "no." I stopped the vote. I explained to them in words they could understand, that Gate had no way of generating money other than borrowing it, and that we were highly leveraged. But that we also had tremendous credibility with the banks: we could borrow more, because of our track record. And that we had to borrow more to expand, because they could not generate enough money through earnings to expand.

I reminded them that Gate had been leveraged since Day One—there had never been any money—and there was no other way to expand at the pace that we had been expanding for the last twenty-some-odd years. And that's the way we were going to expand, now and in the future. That we had many advantages of being structured like we were, that being highly leveraged at the bank was a disadvantage, and that we had to learn to live with it.

I said, "Now we can buy this plant for less money than it's worth, we're in that business already, and we are going to buy the damn plant. Now we are going to vote again." We voted around the room, this time in a clockwise motion. The vote was unanimous that we buy the Houston plant.

We decided to offer them a million dollars; and if they took it, fine, and if they didn't, that was alright, too. They took it. Jack McMann, a Houdaille-Duval employee, is still the manager, and we have done well there. The first year, we almost made our million dollars back. We are now operating six concrete plants in Jacksonville, Florida; Houston, Texas; Monroeville, Alabama; Oxford, North Carolina; Lexington, Kentucky and Nashville, Tennessee. There are more than 800 employees working in this division. It is being expertly run by Joe Luke and Benny Cleghorn.

In this country today, I really think there are two kinds of businessmen. There's the kind that have been through the Depression, and it's left its mark on them and they're very cautious. They're afraid to go in debt. They are always looking over their shoulder, expecting another

Depression to slip up on them at any time. The other kind is a businessman who started after the Depression, and he looks on the ability to borrow money as a resource that should be used. And I fall in the latter group. I've always thought that as long as we bought assets that produced more revenue than the cost of money, that we should be highly leveraged.

The trap is, that if you buy assets that are not worth more than you are paying for them, and things start turning against you, and you're highly leveraged, the whole company could come down like a house of cards, because your exposure is multiplied the more you are leveraged.

Another pitfall which many businessmen have experienced is reflected in the following story.

Several years ago in a south Georgia town where most of the spirit and pride was directed toward the local high school football team, there was a citizen who took extreme interest in this team. He went to every practice session as well as attending all the games. He became so familiar with all the team members that he was asked by the local radio station to sit with them in the pressbox high above the field for purposes of identifying the players.

As the season progressed, he became more involved with the broadcast. It got to the point where he considered himself a sportscaster rather than a spotter, and on occasion he was allowed to talk on the radio briefly. When the biggest rival of the year came to town for their annual battle, he was allowed to announce a few plays.

In the second half, with the score deadlocked at 7 to 7, he was announcing when the following occurred: The ball was centered to the quarterback. The quarterback spun around and handed off to the running back, who went off tackle. At this point, the novice announcer was very excited, reporting in his own style: "Leroy breaks the line of scrimmage, sidesteps the linebacker, swings to the right and is in the clear down the sidelines. He is at midfield... down to the forty... now at the thirty... oh no! he is down by self-tackleization!"

And so, from his bird's eye view of the playing field of human strife, our would-be sportscaster gave the language of business, as well as football, a much-needed new word, never before spoken in the English language— self-tackleization.

Self-tackleization is the mortal enemy of American business today and causes far more casualties than do competitions or other economic forces. The cycle of self-tackleization begins with normal enthusiasm and optimism, but later gives way to overconfidence and the feeling of invincibility. Self-tackleization also is brought about by the loss of dedication to hard work and discipline that enabled the business to be successful in the first place. Self-tackleization occurs in all businesses, both small and large. Small businesses are thriving in this country now because they have less overhead and deadwood than large companies, so they can out-operate them in the field or where the company has direct contact with the customer. Small companies also have more flexibility and quicker reaction times than larger companies have.

Self-tackleization is many times brought about by success. The fact is that very few businessmen plan for success. And when it comes they are not prepared to cope with it. Some businessmen equate success with intellect and therefore their egos take over. They develop a corporate swagger, which is a form of self-tackleization.

Over the years I am proud that Gate hasn't been sidetracked by success.

In the summer of 1982, we bought four stations in Atlanta, and at about the same time, bought twenty-two stations from Charter Oil Company. Those stations were located in Tennessee, Kentucky, Virginia, West Virginia, Georgia, and South Carolina. I wrote the following self-explanatory letter to everyone in our company:

TO: All Gate Employees

FROM: Herb Peyton

Most of you will recall two years ago in the summer of 1980 when we made the Houdaille acquisition. I am sure you will remember how tough the transition period was and what hard times we all had that summer. Now comes the summer of '82. Again we are involved up to our necks in a major acquisition. This time it is even more difficult, in some respects, because it is spread out over a six state area rather than in Florida.

All of our soldiers are on the front line. All our financial resources are committed. Just as in the Houdaille acquisition, we have no reserves. I am calling on everyone in the company for an extra effort. You can expect to have strained milk for the rest of the summer.

The Charter acquisition is a good fit for Gate. It is also a tremendous opportunity and challenge to us. We are excited about this project. If you are not, I suspect you are working for the wrong company. After things settle down, I'm going to do something nice for you.

Sincerely yours,
Herb Peyton
H. H. Peyton
President

We all worked like hell that summer. The letter got the desired results.

Epping Forest is a fifty-eight acre estate on the east bank of the St. Johns River, directly across from Ortega. Built in 1927 by Alfred E. duPont, it originally consisted of an elegant 25,000-square-foot mansion, formal gardens, and an elaborate private marina. In 1972, this prestigious estate was sold to Raymond Mason, president of the Charter Oil Company, for his private residence.

In the spring of 1984 Gate bought Epping Forest. Charter, a Jacksonville-based company, was facing bankruptcy. Raymond Mason owned Epping Forest personally, but he had a couple of out-of-city bank mortgages on it. They were pressuring him and he decided to sell Epping Forest before Charter went into bankruptcy. He put out the word that the price was $10 million. He needed to move very quickly on the sale.

The problem was that Epping had to be completely rezoned as a Planned Unit Development to permit it to be used for anything other than large residential lots. I think most developers were reluctant to buy it without rezoning, which would have taken time.

I struck a deal with Raymond Mason; we bought it for $8 million cash. We didn't have a sales contract; we agreed on the price, the lawyers worked most of that night, and we closed the next morning.

We decided Epping Forest should become a yacht club. Our plan was to put a fine restaurant in the mansion, preserve the formal gardens, expand the marina, and put in a plush fitness center, tennis courts and a residential community. This sounds easy, but it turned out to be a dogfight. It took us a year to get rezoned.

I never did understand why anybody was against it. What we planned to do was certainly the highest and best use for this grand old estate. I was naive enough to think when we started that everybody would welcome the Epping Forest Yacht Club as a tremendous asset for the City of Jacksonville, but such was not the case. A few of the neighbors called me a land baron, and picketed in front of Epping Forest several times.

We got into a fight with City Council about the rezoning, and for the first time I was really exposed to city politics. It was quite educational for me and very frustrating. I found it very hard to understand when a councilman would tell me he was for me, but he was going to vote against me.

However, I think since it's been completed most people like what has been done, and it is a credit to Jacksonville. I am very proud of what we have accomplished at Epping Forest.

Today our club division includes: the Ponte Vedra Inn and Club; Epping Forest Yacht Club and The Deerwood Club. This division is ably run by Z. Mincek.

Gate acquired Blount Island and the facilities which had been built in the early 1970s by a joint venture between Westinghouse and Tenneco. Westinghouse was in a joint venture because of their ability to build generating plants, Tenneco because of their ability in shipbuilding. Their plan had been to build offshore nuclear generating plants, to be put off the coast to generate electricity.

Blount Island was really nothing more than a muck-filled swamp when they bought it from the Jacksonville Port Authority. They spent $125 million on Blount Island, taking all the muck off the soil and filling with good material, building 600,000 square feet of buildings, a complete utility system, sewerage, and water.

In 1978 they erected a gantry crane, one of the largest in the world, at a cost of $16 million. It is nearly 400 feet high, 675 feet wide, and will lift loads up to 900 metric tons. Their plan to build offshore nuclear generating plants was good. However, it didn't work for two reasons.

One was the energy crisis. The price of oil came down and the economics didn't work as well. The second reason was tremendous problems with permits. There were several other factors, but it just didn't all come together.

In the late 1970s, Westinghouse bought Tenneco out of the joint venture, and in the early 1980s Westinghouse decided the offshore nuclear generating plants were not a viable project. They decided to put Blount Island on the market for $75 million cash, and hired the brokerage firm of Cushman Wakefield.

Shipyards were having a tough time all over the world, especially in the States, because labor was so much cheaper in many parts of the world. There were no buyers. Westinghouse was not willing to sell outparcels, take a purchase money mortgage, or anything. Blount Island stayed on the market for a couple of years, and there were still no buyers.

I called the Westinghouse office in Pittsburgh, made an appointment, and flew up there by myself on the Gate plane. They picked me up at the airport and took me to their headquarters in downtown Pittsburgh. We rode the elevator up about thirty floors and had a meeting with three Westinghouse officers. They were at first very polite and cordial.

I offered to joint venture Blount Island with them, and

they said "no. " I then told them Blount Island was really a shipyard; that shipyards were not doing well in this country, and it had to be sold off in parcels or leased or developed, and their sales approach would not work. They sat there and looked and did not agree or disagree.

Then I told them if they were not willing to do one of those things, the only buyer would be a land speculator and that's what I was. And I told them further, they had a white elephant on their hands, and I would give them $15 million cash for Blount Island.

One vice president sitting over in the corner had had very little to say up to this point. He seemed to be kind of in charge. He stood up and said, "Mr. Peyton, I tell you what we'll do for you. We'll take you back to the airport right now." And he told a man to take me to the airport. On the way, the man said "Well, we'll talk it over and I'll call you Monday morning"; and I never heard a word from them.

About two months later I called them on a pretense of talking about something else. I asked Allen Wood, the man who had taken me to the airport, "By the way, whatever happened to my offer on Blount Island?" He said that was discussed Monday morning at the staff meeting, and it was decided my offer didn't even justify a phone call to Florida. And I said "Okay, that's fine, but nevertheless, my analysis of that island is correct, and when it all shakes out, that's where it will wind up."

About two months later, I got a call from Allen Wood, and they wanted to meet me in Atlanta to talk about Blount Island. After several weeks, we came to an agreement. We paid about $17 million for Blount Island. What had changed during that period, I later found out, was they had a directive from the Board of Directors to sell Blount Island during the 1985 fiscal year, and Gate was their only buyer.

They had wanted $75 million for that island, which had cost them $125 million to construct, yet we wound up paying only about $17 million for it. We later sold the gantry crane to the Chinese for $3 million. The truth was—when it all shook out—Westinghouse wanted to get rid of Blount Island badly. It was just a case of a big company wanting out, and our cash offer being the best deal around at that time.

One of the reasons Westinghouse sold Blount Island so cheap was that the ad valorum taxes were over $1 million a year. We were successful in getting the taxes reduced to $600,000. The local newspaper reported we had gotten favorable treatment from the Tax Assessor's office, and intimated we had done it through questionable means. They tried to make a scandal out of it; of course, it wasn't. They got the FBI involved, we got Walter Arnold involved, and it all worked out. The fact is, it was still assessed at more than double what we paid.

Blount Island is fine property because of a feature desirable in all real estate—it is unique. Nothing else on the east coast of this country compares to Blount Island. It is a tremendous facility: its direct access to the ocean and the absence of overhead structures between it and the ocean, its proximity to the metropolitan area of Jacksonville, and the improvements on the island, make it one of the best maritime properties in the United States today. This division is well run by Jack Lueders and Tom Mantie.

Blount Island is now leased to the United States Marine Corps. The Blount Island Command is a permanent Marine base and the world headquarters for the Maritime Pre-positioning Forces (MPF). The MPF reduces military response time from weeks to days by pre-positioning the bulk of the equipment and thirty days of supplies for a 16,000-man Marine brigade aboard specifically designed, strategically deployed ships. The MPF is a vital part of this country's defense and proved its worth during Desert Storm.

We later bought the Gulf Life Tower and the surrounding twenty acres on the Southbank of downtown Jacksonville. In many ways the acquisition was a replay of Blount Island. The Tower was owned by American General Corporation of Houston, and for almost three years had been on the market for thirty million dollars. We purchased the 542,000-square-foot, 28-floor tower, parking garage and hotel on nearly twenty acres. The Welton Becket-designed building had been a landmark in Jacksonville for many years. The truth was that little had been done to it in nearly thirty years.

For tax reasons, it was necessary for them to sell the Tower in the calendar year 1993. It was already October, so what they needed was a buyer that could close for cash—and fast. Gate could do all of the above because of our unique structure, so we were able to buy the Tower for less than one-third of what they were asking. We closed in thirty days.

When we bought the Tower, the occupancy rate was forty percent. It is now over ninety percent. We have restored the building, now called the Riverplace Tower, to its former prominence. I believe that this property is the finest riverfront location in Jacksonville.

The Riverplace Tower division is very professionally managed by Jeremy Smith and Jim Citrano.

Today there are over 200 Gate service stations located in six southeastern states. Service stations are still our core business. This division, called Gate Marketing, is run by Mitchell Rhodes and Wayne Levitt.

Diversification was forced on Gate by the energy crisis and it led us into many exciting ventures. It is by no means easy to diversify from a core business. I can compare diversification to canoeing down a fast river with many unknowns around the bends. It worked for us because the Brothers were all in the same boat paddling together.

Chapter Thirteen

The Money Changers

I have a lot of dealings with bankers now, and I have spent a lot of time with them over the years. They are a fascinating group to me. I find them to be nervous and highly suspicious and by nature very inquisitive. Bankers amaze me in that they are all as alike as crows on a limb; they think alike, they dress alike in their dark suits and black shoes, they smile, and they're friendly.

The problem I have with bankers really is two-fold. First, bankers, if they ever help you, as Hugh Jones did in the acquisition of Houdaille-Duval, and as Billy Walker did in the acquisition of SWD, always want to remind you, "Well, you remember what I did for you."

Hugh Jones would use a word on me that I thought was unfair. He used to tell me that he "enabled" Gate to do this and to do that and so forth. And as a result of Barnett's deal, they always expected Gate to pay a premium after that, because of what they had done for us in the past.

But this has not lead to the demise of my friendship with Hugh Jones; I understand him. He's a pure banker, and cannot help it—he has a mindset when it comes to these matters.

This is an ongoing problem, because I'm out trying to borrow money for a new venture, and the bankers are saying "Well, remember what we did for you back then," to justify charging a higher rate.

The second problem I have with bankers is that when they once go out on a limb for Gate, and really put it all on the line, and then we pay them back, we get it worked out, but they're not willing to do it again. They seem to take a deep breath and say, "I'm glad that's over." I remember a few years ago, the C&S Bank in Atlanta made the statement to one of the other banks — and they were very serious — that banking for Gate Petroleum was like having a Chinese fire drill every two months, and they were just worn out with it.

Another thing that has hurt our banking over the years is that these bankers have made so much money that they've gotten the wrinkles out of their bellies and are just not willing to put it all on the line anymore. They've gone conservative.

But we have always had a tremendous rapport with the bankers over the years, as evidenced by the fact that we were able to borrow more than $100 million from them. The reason we've always had good rapport is we told them the truth about most things and we understood what they were all about.

Bankers are really just money changers. The scriptures tell us that Jesus ran them out of the temple. A bank's primary function is taking deposits which they typically horde and making loans, and that's fine. In actuality, they contribute only through the successes of businesses they loan money to. Can you imagine running a business where all you have to worry about is whether some sonofabitch is going to pay you?

When we first started doing business at the Barnett Bank, they loved Gate, because we had big cash deposits from our service stations every night. We got along fine. But after we made the Houdaille-Duval acquisition and owed them over $10 million, it seemed they spent a good part of their time trying to figure ways to make money off of us, while we were busy trying to manage a new business that we knew very little about.

I have never begrudged the bankers the interest we had agreed to pay. I deeply resent the additional money they try to trick us out of.

One of their tricks was charging us interest computed daily on a 360-day year. However, they turned around and charged us interest on 365 days (366 days on Leap Year), therefore collecting more money per day. The end result of this was they collected five extra days' interest on us every year. I'll never forget the blank look the Barnett bankers gave me when I confronted them with this. They acted like they were confused and didn't know what I was talking about.

Another one of their classic tricks is that in addition to interest at an agreed rate, they want additional interest if you don't maintain a certain minimum balance in your accounts. I refer to this as paying interest on money you don't borrow, and I have on my office wall a two-page letter from Barnett Bank, trying to explain this additional charge. Nobody that has ever read this letter has been able to tell me how much this amounts to. That is a part of their program—total confusion.

These are just a few of the tricks bankers have in their arsenal. They spend their time in their paneled offices plotting ways to clean our plow, while we are trying to run a business.

Pa told me, when I was a teenager, a banker would loan you an umbrella when the sun is shining but when it started to rain, they wanted it back. Have you ever noticed that people who really need to borrow money have to pay much more for it than some sonofabitch who doesn't really need a loan because he already has a lot of money?

And Uncle Bill, the Old Sonofabitch, used to say that when he died, he would not be concerned about burning in hell. He explained his lack of concern by advancing his theory that the bankers would all be placed up on the front row, because of the money they stole over the years. So, there wouldn't be much heat on the back row where he would be seated.

In spite of all this, I like bankers. As long as bankers don't take themselves too seriously, we get along fine.

—Chapter Fourteen—

Drawing to an Inside Straight

S tockton, Whatley & Davin Company had been a prominent real estate and mortgage company in north Florida for a century when we acquired the SWD Real Estate Division. Our acquisition came about when Boone Pickens attempted a hostile takeover of General American Oil Company of Texas, a Dallas company which owned SWD at the time.

General American went to Phillips Petroleum Company, whom they had known and liked. They asked Phillips to buy General American to prevent the Pickens takeover. Phillips agreed, and it happened in a matter of days, an unbelievably short time for an acquisition of that size.

Phillips paid about $1.3 billion for General American, which had quite a few oil and gas reserves, and they were good ones. The purchase came about so quickly that Phillips had no financing in place for the acquisition. They had close to a billion dollars in the bank, and they borrowed the balance, but they decided after they bought it that they should sell off the parts of General American they didn't want and keep the oil and gas reserves. They decided to sell SWD. This happened in December 1982 and January 1983. The Phillips people came to Jacksonville and toured the holdings, and said it was beautiful property but they were going to sell it because they were not in the land business. Their overall company policy was to stay in the petroleum business or related fields. SWD did not fall into that category and besides, it was over a thousand miles from Bartlesville, Oklahoma.

At that time, we had been buying gasoline from Phillips for over ten years and had very good rapport with the management. As a matter of fact, we were their largest gasoline customer in the world, and we had a contract with them to supply us with all of our petroleum needs.

When all this began unfolding in the winter of 1983, I was watching it very closely, along with everybody else in Jacksonville. At first, I thought Raymond Mason would wind up with SWD, because he had been in the mortgage business years ago, and because he was a master at acquisitions.

I decided to put together a fishing trip and invited my Phillips friends over to go bass fishing that spring. Among them was Pete Morrison, Vice President of Marketing, who had a lot of influence over there. The purpose of this trip was to see if Gate could buy part of SWD.

When all of this came about, Gate didn't have any money. As a matter of fact, we had just bought the Charter stations the summer before, in 1982. We not only had no money, we were $15 million in debt when Pete Morrison told me they had decided to sell SWD. I asked him if they would sell Gate part of it before it was put out to bid, and told him the specific parts I would like to buy. I offered to buy the quadrants of Southside Boulevard and J. Turner Butler Boulevard.

He called me from Bartlesville when he got back and said no, they wanted to sell it all for cash, and he was sorry, there was nothing he could do about that—he couldn't help me.

When spring came, I was still interested, and I got in touch with Henry Luke, who was president of Plantec, a division of Reynolds, Smith, and Hill. Henry Luke is the brother of Joe Luke, who is a Vice President of Gate.

Henry knew what was going on and knew everybody interested in bidding, and he had his own ideas; he was very helpful. I had thought they were going to sell everything for cash, to one buyer. I found out they had turned the sale over to Morgan Stanley of New York and had decided to accept separate bids for the real estate and the mortgage company.

However, each division would cost a tremendous amount of money. So I decided the thing for me to do was go to Bartlesville, Oklahoma. I took the company plane and went out on Sunday afternoon, unannounced, by myself. I called Pete Morrison at home Sunday night and asked him to have breakfast with me early Monday morning.

Pete told me there was nothing he could do to help me, but he would introduce me to the man who was handling the sale for Phillips Petroleum. We went over to the Phillips offices and he introduced me to a financial vice president named Gene Bonnell. I had never met Mr. Bonnell, but he knew I was a Phillips customer.

By this time I had decided the only way I could possibly buy SWD was if Phillips Petroleum would sign—in other words, guarantee a bank loan for Gate Petroleum Company. I thought they might consider this because after all, they did extend us a lot of credit for gasoline, and we were into them for several million dollars at all times, because of the ten day float.

Gene Bonnell indicated to me that Phillips probably would not do that; it was strictly a cash sale. Then I asked him if he would advise me how to go about bidding for SWD. He was very blunt with me. He said his advice to me was not to bid, because there were 142 companies interested in this acquisition, and they were big companies, and he knew the price range they were going to bid it up to, and at those prices it wasn't a good buy. Besides that, he said, it was much too big for Gate; at those price levels it would probably bankrupt Gate Petroleum.

At the conclusion of our meeting, I asked, "Well, can I submit a bid?" And he said, "You can do anything you want to, but I can tell you now it will not work." So I remember I headed back to Jacksonville, and one of my friends from Phillips Petroleum took me back to the airport. I was quite upset and I told him I didn't understand why, as close as Gate and Phillips were over the years, when they got ready to sell something I was treated like somebody off the street. I had to bid for it just like anybody else, and I didn't get any consideration or help from Phillips Petroleum Company. I didn't think that was fair. Bob Elson, who had taken me to the airport, didn't let his shirttail hit his backside before he got back and told them what I'd said.

But at any rate, back in Florida I met with the Brothers, and we came within a hair of saying "the hell with it, we're not going to bid." But after thinking about it for awhile, I decided it was like playing poker back in Kentucky. We didn't have to ante anything to bid, and it's true we were drawing to an inside straight, but we had nothing to lose by bidding.

So I called back to Bartlesville and told them I wanted to bid and to tell me what to do to submit my bid. They put me in touch with Bill Aberly. Bill lived in Jacksonville; I had known him to speak to over the years. He was President of SWD.

I remember I went down to see Bill Aberley and took Jeremy Smith, Financial Vice President of Gate, with me. Jeremy was embarrassed to go down to Bill's office. In fact, he didn't much want to go. And we went down that morning and Bill was polite to me, but he said Phillips had called him and he said, "I understand you're the biggest Phillips customer in the state of Florida." I said, "No, we are not the biggest in Florida, we're the biggest gasoline customer they've got in the world."

I remember walking down the hall at SWD and there would be thirty people in the meeting room with dark suits on, and briefcases, and I'd ask, "Who is that?" And they would say, "Well, that's the group from First of Boston, or that's the Sun Bank" from down in Orlando—companies were in there from California and New York and Texas, and in large groups, and there I was with Jeremy, and he didn't want to be there. It was very intimidating.

We talked to the NCNB Bank, and they agreed if Phillips Petroleum signed the note, they would loan us the money—there would be no problem. So we went to work on preparing the bid. The Gate Petroleum people who worked on the bid preparation were Joe Luke, Jeremy Smith, and me. The outsiders we had working on it were Henry Luke, Dave Foster, and Leland Burpee — six people.

The first thing we did was tour the properties, which took all day. They conducted a regular tour for all bidders, in a van. We visited Deerwood and Deerwood Center, the four quadrants at the corner of J. Turner Butler and Southside Boulevards, Ponte Vedra, the Regency property, Guana Lake, all the beach frontage around Ponte Vedra, and miscellaneous properties. The six of us met the next Saturday morning at the Gate Office Conference Room— the war room—and went around the table with each asset, got a consensus of what each asset was worth, and used that for the base.

When we got that totaled up, it came out to a little over

$100 million. We decided the wholesale price was worth sixty percent of the retail price, and that was our bid. Now during that period, I remember wanting to bid $66 million, which I thought was significant because Phillips trademark was Phillips 66. I thought it might hit an emotional nerve for them because of the Phillips name.

But the others convinced me that price was too high, we should bid sixty million, which we did. The bid was not a cash bid like they wanted; it was a bid predicated on two things: one was they would sign the note guaranteeing the sixty million, and two, that Phillips would get ten percent of all the sales that we made, thereafter. In other words, if we sold some property for a million dollars, they would get ten percent of a million dollars. During those last few weeks it was very hectic and we were about the last bidder in. We had been the last bidders who toured the property.

During that period we were about the only small company in the bidding. Bill Aberley, whom I got to know pretty well during those days, was awfully nice to me. He told the Morgan Stanley people in New York, when they were trying to get his opinion on who the likely winners of the bidding process would be, "don't forget Peyton, because he doesn't know what anything's worth, so he's liable to bid anything."

Bill Sharpstone was a young fellow who worked for Morgan Stanley and lived in New York. He had several meetings during that period with all the people involved, including me, about who the likely winners were. When the most likely buyers were discussed, Bill Sharpstone said to Bill Aberley and to others, "Don't forget the Lone Ranger," talking about Gate. Their whole attitude was that we were kind of a joke.

The bid was to be in New York before Monday, May 15, 1983. I called Sharpstone and asked him if he had any last minute advice. He said, and I will never forget, "Now is the time to be bold." So it was in that spirit that we sealed our bid and sent it by Federal Express to New York. Although we had absolutely no money, and our chances were minimal, it seemed to me I had worked all my life for this, and this was it.

During those hectic days while we had been putting our bid together, and it was obvious we had no money, Henry Luke and I had decided the best thing for Gate to do was to get involved in the bid with somebody else, and we had tried to do that with several people; one was the Sun Bank and another was Hugh Culverhouse. Nobody was interested in bidding with us. Henry said the best thing for me to do was to get in with a group from Jacksonville who were bidding. He was a little bit familiar with who was in there and believed they had the clout. He knew they'd been to Bartlesville, and he thought they probably had a good chance.

I knew most of the people in that group, had seen them at various business and social events, and had hinted to them that I'd like to get into that group, but they didn't respond. Henry said, "Well look, I know Steve Wilson well, and Jack Demetree and Martin Stein. Let me see what I can do." And I said, "Fine."

He called Steve Wilson. Steve said, "Well, let me talk to Jack Demetree and I'll get back to you." Henry pointed out to him that I was Phillip's biggest customer and it might be helpful. So Steve called Jack Demetree and Jack said "We don't want Peyton; we've done all the work now, and we're going to win it, and we don't need any more partners." So that word was conveyed to Henry Luke.

These people were some of the business elite of Jacksonville, many of them were from the Ortega area, and they really did have the clout, without any question, and the credit, and the credibility, to pull this thing off. They were the logical winners of this process.

The principals in that group were Steve Wilson, Jack Demetree, and Martin Stein. Steve went to Bartlesville twice and met with those Phillips people, who were very impressed with him—they told me they were, when I went over there. Some of that group made statements around town before the bidding that they were going to get those assets; and they really thought they were, because they had gone to such trouble and expense in putting together that bid.

Theirs was a strong bid, no question about it, and they had the wherewithal to do it, but they had made some bad mistakes in their bid. They didn't offer to pay all cash; they had a kicker on the end very much like ours, in which Phillips would participate and share in the profits. The worst mistake they made was in not turning in three bids: one for the whole company, one for the real estate division, and one for the mortgage company. If they had, they would have won the real estate division, although they probably would not have won the mortgage company.

That one error tripped them up. There had been discussion among that group about doing that, but they had decided, no, we're going to win the whole thing, we've got it made, we don't want part.

While all this was going on, I was preparing to go on a mountain climbing trip to Mount McKinley in Alaska, and I had trained for this trip for almost a year. I had bought two thousand dollars worth of gear. I had gotten my plane ticket and we had hired a guide. I was going with Ted Kilpatrick, and this was the first big-league mountain I was to be on. I was all hyped up to go, supposed to leave on Friday the 19th.

The bidding date was Monday the 15th, four days before the climbing trip. Early Tuesday afternoon about 1 p. m., I got a phone call from New York. Simon Orme, an officer of Morgan Stanley, was on the phone. I remember he spoke to me with an English accent and he asked me if I could come to New York; and I asked him, "For what purpose?"

He said that we were the high bidder on SWD; and I said, "Well, I can come right now. I can be at the airport in about thirty minutes; how would that do?" And then he said no, could we come up on Thursday.

I canceled my trip to Alaska, and we flew up on our plane to New York. We met with the Morgan Stanley people in their offices in downtown Manhattan.

For Gate to be the successful bidder was the long shot, and the odds had to be several hundred to one, at best.

SWD Mortgage Company, the financial part of SWD, was worth about $100 million. It was very easy to analyze how much it was worth, and a lot of big mortgage companies were bidding for it and they were all bidding in about that range. The First Bank of Boston wanted very much to be in Florida. They decided to pay more than it was worth to assure that they would get the mortgage company, and they bid $125 million.

That bid, along with our $60 million for the property, was $185 million, and that was five to ten million dollars higher than any of the single bids. Most of the bidders bid for the whole company, and those bid ranges ran from $150 million to $180 million. So we rode the coattails of First of

Boston, and because they bid high, it made our bid work; the combination of the two was best for Phillips. Gate still had one problem with the bid—no money—which had been our problem all along.

Morgan Stanley had made a serious mistake in structuring the bid process for SWD. They should have separated the bidding for Ponte Vedra Inn and Club from the real estate. The resort owners were scared of the real estate, and the real estate developers were scared of the resort. So Morgan Stanley eliminated a lot of potential bidders, particularly for Ponte Vedra Inn and Club.

When we were called to New York to meet with the Morgan Stanley people, we had prepared to show we were solvent enough and financially able to pay back the $60 million that we were going to borrow with Phillips' guarantee. We had quite extensive projections made, balance sheets, and so forth. When we got up there in the meeting, it was very formal and in the conference room. We were about half way through the presentation when Joe Fogg, who ran the office for Morgan Stanley, called me out of the office and said, "This isn't going to work."

I said, "What the hell do you mean?" He said, "Phillips isn't going to guarantee your loan." He said, "You've either got the money or you haven't—they're not going to guarantee anybody's money on this deal. This was a cash bid, and you were told that before you ever bid. You can come up with the money, or you lose."

I said, "Well, why won't they guarantee the credit? We're customers of Phillips, and they've been giving us credit for years." And he said, "You don't understand. Phillips' whole idea was to liquidate these assets, and they want their cash money. They don't want any outparcels sold, any leases, purchase money mortgage, or anything except the cash; and that is the only way they are going to do it."

And he also said Phillips was scared to death of Florida real estate, and they weren't about to guarantee anything that had to do with Florida real estate. I said "That's fine, we'll come up with the money." This was on a Thursday, and he said, "I'll give you to next Monday night to raise the $60 million." I said, "That's fine; we'll borrow the money and leave Phillips out of it."

So we got in our plane and came home, and on the way home everybody was very discouraged, because we did not know how we could raise $60 million.

When we had decided to bid on the SWD real estate, I knew our chances were slim and none. In order for this to come about, several things had to fall in place at the right time. We got home from New York on Thursday night. There was nothing to do but start hitting the banks, and on Friday morning, without an appointment, Joe Luke, Jeremy Smith, and I walked into Billy Walker's office at the Atlantic Bank.

I told him we were the high bidder on the SWD Real Estate Division and that we needed to borrow $60 million and we had four days to raise it. Billy could not believe that we had been the successful bidder.

This was way beyond Atlantic's loan limits at the time, and it would involve getting two other banks in addition to the Atlantic to commit. To accomplish this in four days, two of which fell on the weekend, is an almost impossible banking feat. We were successful in raising the money because of one man, Billy J. Walker, President of Atlantic Bank.

We had been banking with Billy for several years. We

got Billy's attention because of our excellent relationship with Atlantic Bank, but also because Billy knew the value of those properties, although at this time in early 1983, the interest rates were still high. The prime was 11 1/2 or 12 percent, and real estate was still very stagnant everywhere, and particularly in Jacksonville.

Billy lined us up to visit other banks in the South because the loan was too big for his bank. That weekend we flew up on our plane to Atlanta and visited the C & S Bank people; we made a presentation in the airplane hangar at the airport. NCNB came up Sunday, and we showed them the properties, and they talked back and forth on the phone to their headquarters in Charlotte. We worked on it until, in the middle of the afternoon Monday, we had a meeting in my office with the NCNB people. The manager of the Florida operation, Ed Brown, told me they would not be able to participate in this loan. I was devastated, because it seemed like this time we had hit a stone wall.

It was after all, if you review the loan, primarily for raw real estate, and although the Deerwood Club and the Ponte Vedra Club were in there, they didn't make much money. A raw real estate loan is very hard to finance, and this came at a time when the banks had been severely burned back in the early 1970s on the real estate investment trusts, and banks were still very leery of real estate loans.

Well, time was running out, we hadn't been able to raise the money, and we were trying all different ways, none of which seemed to work. By this time, we were all exhausted, as we had been working night and day since the previous Tuesday.

It was quite a shock that Gate got the bid, because nobody even knew Gate was bidding, and the "Old Boy" group in Jacksonville that had bid was shocked and disappointed, of course, because they had worked very hard and spent a lot of money, apparently feeling very confident they were going to win.

After the word got out, Bill Aberley said he got about six or eight phone calls that weekend, asking who in the hell was Gate, and where did they get the money? Steve Wilson called Phillips Petroleum Company after it was announced that Gate got the bid, and offered them $80 million for the real estate division. They told Steve they didn't do business that way, that Gate had bid $60 million, and if we couldn't come up with the money, they'd be glad to talk to him.

Phillips Petroleum had been used to bidding offshore oil drilling prices and was very formal in its bidding processes. Since we had been their customer for years, they were loyal and honorable to Gate.

On that Monday afternoon when we were running out of time to find the financing, I called Phillips in Bartlesville and told Gene Bonnell I had gotten it just about put together and I needed an extension on time. He explained to me he was under a lot of pressure out there; people had offered him a lot more money than we had agreed to pay; and he would give us twenty-four hours and that's all. And he wanted it clearly understood if we didn't come up with the money by Tuesday at five o'clock, they were going to sell it to somebody else for more money.

I told him I understood that, I thought it was fair, and I'd be back in touch with him on Tuesday. And we continued to work on it. Billy Walker really came to bat for us then, putting a lot of pressure on C&S Bank in Atlanta.

We had a meeting in Billy Walker's conference room

Tuesday afternoon about two o'clock; they had set up a conference call on the speaker phone with C&S Bank in Atlanta and the NCNB Bank in Charlotte. They drilled us for about thirty minutes about our plans. They did not want to go into the deal, but Billy continued to pressure them. By this time it was three o'clock and we had only two hours left.

The Gate people were asked to leave the room at about four o'clock and Billy stayed in there and talked to the bankers. I can remember walking out of the conference room and Joe Luke saying, "This will never work. We're running out of time. We're not going to make it." They talked for another thirty minutes or an hour on the phone.

Billy came out at about four-thirty and said, "Everything is agreed!" He sent a Telex to Morgan Stanley in New York, guaranteeing the $60 million, and I called Gene Bonnell in Bartlesville. By the time we got the Telex off, we had less than twenty minutes to spare. I went home and got the first good night's sleep I'd had in about a week.

When the other banks had tried to break and run, Billy had stood fast like a soldier. He had refused to take no for an answer, and finally had gotten them to agree by sheer worriation. The fact is that Billy Walker put his banking reputation and credibility in the southeastern United States on the line for Gate Petroleum Company. He had gone far above and beyond the call of duty as our banker, and I will never forget his all-out effort when all the chips were on the table.

Billy Walker has been Gate's main banker for the last quarter of a century, and during that time we have had good times and bad times. But the fact is, he is the best and most able banker in Florida.

Sometime after we purchased SWD, when the smoke of

battle had cleared, Billy Walker made the statement to me that I had some divine intervention in the SWD acquisition. That to me was a profound statement, because I had the exact same feeling all along. As a matter of fact, I had the feeling before we bid that we were going to be successful, although most of the Brothers didn't take our bid seriously and thought we were wasting our time.

I sincerely believe that God had a hand in it, but I have never understood whether He was trying to help Newboy or whether he was just looking for a caretaker for Ponte Vedra that would do it justice. I still don't know the answer as to why God intervened, but I will always be absolutely convinced that He did.

The next week we flew to New York and put up a $6 million binder, which was ten percent of the purchase price, and we had until the first of June to close. Now when the word circulated around Jacksonville, Florida, that we had gotten the bid, there was a lot of talk we'd never be able to close; there was some talk that if we were able to close, we'd have to liquidate everything almost immediately to make it; and many people said that it would bankrupt us.

It was 1983, the economy was still flat, and interest rates were still high. It was obvious we had our work cut out for us and we had one chance—to sell property fast, for cash. With SWD, Gate had a total debt of $75 million at twelve percent interest.

I remember the following Saturday morning the Brothers met in the Gate conference room. There were about fourteen of us, and I told them everything about the SWD acquisition, and what our plans were, as some of them had not been involved. I broke the interest down: so much a month, so much a week, so much a day; and I remember the blackboard showed it was $25,000 a day and $17.36 a minute, twenty-four hours a day.

George Nail listened to all this and he made a very astute observation. He said, "Well, may I make a suggestion?" I said, "Yes." He said, "I suggest you call New York and tell them to keep the $6 million binder and let's us go back to doing what we know how to do." I rejected George's suggestion.

We stopped all expenditures in the field, we kept our gasoline prices up, and we didn't spend any money for anything for a year. In other words, we battened down the hatches and got ready for the storm we knew was forthcoming.

When we finally did get to the closing, I can remember sitting around the Atlantic Bank conference room. There were about a dozen lawyers, there must have been twenty bankers from the three banks involved—the Atlantic, the NCNB, and the C&S. The closing took most of the day. I can remember while we were waiting for the various documents to be signed, one of those young bankers made the comment that his bank gave us a fifty-fifty chance, at best, that this acquisition would bankrupt us.

Bryant Skinner had said, back when I had talked with him about joining us in the bidding, "No, I don't want to go into that." He had predicted that because of all of the dust that had been stirred up, we would have some sales at first, maybe even $20 million worth of real estate. But he said, "After that, you won't be able to sell any real estate and the debt will bankrupt you."

We went to work. We knew there was interest in parts of SWD; in fact, the other bidders got in touch with us and expressed interest in various parts. They would gather in our war room and we would always say, "Now before we start, you get exactly the same terms we got: none. Anything we talk about will be for cash and quick closing." And we started to sell property.

—Chapter Fifteen—

Ponte Vedra

When we bought the SWD real estate we had to start selling assets, fast, because we were paying about $25,000 a day interest and our days were numbered. We eventually sold Guana Island to the State for $49 million and took that pressure off, but for a year, there was tremendous pressure on everybody in the company. At times we were right down to the waterline.

During that time prospective buyers kept showing interest in the Ponte Vedra Inn and Club. The first offer was $10 million, and when we didn't respond to that, they increased it. There were six or eight serious purchasers that kept coming back.

It became obvious early on that one of our most salable assets was the Ponte Vedra Inn and Club, so the plan was to sell Ponte Vedra quickly. Now that was everybody else's plan—the bankers' and the Brothers'. I had no intention of selling Ponte Vedra; and I didn't say anything, but I knew if we ever closed on SWD, Ponte Vedra would never be sold. I remembered when I moved to Neptune Beach from Kentucky, the first time I saw Ponte Vedra, the tremendous impression it made on me. I thought it was the prettiest place I'd ever seen in my life. Therefore I had a great emotional feeling and respect for the Ponte Vedra Inn and Club, and still do.

During this talk of selling Ponte Vedra, I kept quiet and still, because I didn't want to get the bankers or anybody upset, but I was determined that sale would never come about. Ponte Vedra Inn and Club is really, in at least my estimation, one of the finest assets in northeast Florida—not strictly from the moneymaking point of view, but from the standpoint of pride in ownership and potential appreciation.

There were many emotional meetings back in the Gate war room about Ponte Vedra, and about our plight in general, which was that we were quickly running out of money. About two months after we bought SWD, Joe Luke came in my office and sat on the couch. He looked completely exhausted and whipped, and he said, "We're not going to make it. We're going to sell and sell and sell, and when the selling stops, we're still going to owe a fortune, and it will break us."

And I said, "What the hell are you talking about?" He said, "We're selling some real estate now, but when the real estate sales dry up, we will still have thirty or forty million dollars of debt, and it will bankrupt us."

And I said, "Well, Joe, I don't think that's right." But he and I both knew that the whole thing probably would swing on Ponte Vedra. I was trying to put off the sale of Ponte Vedra and he was trying to hurry it up. I remember at one meeting in the board room, Joe stood up and hollered the only reason I liked Ponte Vedra was because I liked to go out there and be waited on. And I admitted to that, but nevertheless, I didn't want to sell.

Jeremy Smith, who had come down here from Boston, worked for Barnett Bank before we hired him for the specific purpose of watching the bankers. He still breathes, thinks, and acts like a banker, even today. Another of Golden Boy's valuable attributes is that he is so stingy he wouldn't give a nickel to see a pissant eat a bale of hay. Jeremy insisted that Ponte Vedra should be sold, immediately, or we were going to be in serious trouble.

The leaders in this Sell Ponte Vedra Brigade were Joe
Luke and Jeremy Smith, but all the Brothers, just about
without exception, wanted to sell. I stalled and delayed.
Finally, after they kept harassing me about it and it was at
the point where I couldn't walk down the hall without one
of them jumping me, I said, "I tell you what we'll do. We'll
have a meeting of the Brothers, and we'll vote. You give
your pitch. Jeremy and Joe can tell the reasons it should be
sold. I will state my case as to why it should not be sold.
Then we'll leave the room and we'll let the Brothers vote."

We met in the Gate war room and Joe and Jeremy gave
an emotional plea based on financial facts, why Ponte
Vedra should be sold and must be sold now. Their
presentation was organized, it was completely thought out,
and it was right on target.

I told the Brothers that Ponte Vedra represented to this
company something that could not be bought at any price.
I told them when we bid on SWD and were successful,
there were many people in Duval County who said we
would not be able to close. They said if we did close, at
minimum we'd have to liquidate everything, and Ponte
Vedra would be sold in thirty days. And their position was
that Ponte Vedra should never be owned by Gate
Petroleum Company anyway. And to me, it represented
more than a financial asset; it was a status symbol for Gate
Petroleum Company. We could operate it—not only
operate it, but operate it better than it had ever been
operated before.

And I told them that I was proud of it, and that it would
appreciate probably faster than any other asset we had.
And that it was true that it was making very little money,
but at least it was a cash-generating asset, unlike most of

the SWD properties, and it did generate some cash flow. And that it should not, in my opinion, be sold.

We left the room, and you could walk down the hall and hear them in there arguing and hollering among themselves for at least an hour or an hour and a half. It was a tough decision, because we were hurting. We were stretched out and the interest was eating us alive and something had to give. Ponte Vedra could have been sold immediately, for cash, which would have taken all the pressure off of us. At one point, they called me back in the room for clarification. They wanted to know if I was recommending Ponte Vedra never be sold, or just not be sold now. I said I just didn't want it sold now—and probably never, but certainly not now.

The vote came in—twelve Brothers voted; Joe Luke, Jeremy Smith, and I didn't vote—and the vote was seven to five, and I just barely won. Joe and Jeremy claimed that the whole thing was rigged, because they were out of the room when the others called me back in the war room. Joe and Jeremy claimed when I went back in I either threatened them, or promised them something, or both.

Nevertheless, I told them that the Ponte Vedra matter had been decided by democratic process and I didn't want it ever brought up again—I never again wanted to hear anybody suggest we sell Ponte Vedra. They felt better and it got them off my back. And they have abided by that, ever since.

What Jeremy and Joe and all the other twelve who voted didn't know, was if I had lost twelve to zero, I would still have held Ponte Vedra until the bankers threatened foreclosure.

The interest payments were tough, and we had trouble

meeting some of them; we paid our interest monthly, and there were times when we didn't think we were going to make it.

Now the race began. It was obvious to me the only way Ponte Vedra could be saved was to sell Guana Lake to the State of Florida. I had gone to Tallahassee soon after the closing for this purpose. I knew the State had held some discussions with SWD about putting the Guana tract on the CARL (Conservation and Recreational Lands) list. The State had expressed interest in buying this land years before for a state park, but SWD would never sell it, so I went to Tallahassee to see Elton Gissendanner, who ran the Department of Natural Resources for the State of Florida.

I told him I would consider selling Guana; that I probably was going to sell it either to the State of Florida or to developers; but that I had a tremendous interest load and we couldn't wait a long period of time. He said he wanted two months to decide whether the State was interested in buying it or not, and I said, "Fine, I'll be back over here in two months."

The Guana tract includes 8,000 acres in a heavily wooded area left in its primitive state, and is surrounded by water on three sides. The Intracoastal Waterway is on the west, the Guana River is on the east, and it is some of the most beautiful real estate in northeast Florida, completely natural. Guana is exactly like it was two hundred years ago, heavily wooded with tremendous oaks, hickories, magnolias, and pines.

In two months, the State of Florida did indicate a serious interest in Guana.

We started working on it. The first step was to get on the CARL list. They had to go through all the bureaus and all the legal processes including appraisals.

When we were negotiating for the sale of Guana, I was surprised when the State sent a young man, at least twenty years my junior, over here to negotiate with me. We had lunch down in the golf shop of the Ponte Vedra Inn and Club and after the lunch decided to go upstairs and talk in private in one of the meeting rooms in the Inn, which was about a three-minute walk.

Walking over there, I knew that the next twenty or thirty minutes was going to determine whether or not we would be able to hold on to Ponte Vedra. If Guana did not sell to the State, we had to sell Ponte Vedra, and the Brothers and bankers were becoming very impatient and I had stalled just about as long as I could.

And I also knew that, really, the whole SWD acquisition swung on this conversation, because without the sale of Guana to the State, it would have been a very tough deal. We could have very well bogged down and could have gotten into serious financial trouble. I had worked with the State of Florida for almost a year and had arrived at this point.

Under this tremendous pressure, my mind was racing and the adrenaline was flowing. I can remember very clearly, while walking over to the Inn, trying to size this fellow up. I can remember thinking, "I wonder how tough he is and whether he can be bluffed, and how he's going to hold up when I give him both barrels. I wonder if this man ever played poker. Because that is what we are about to play, and the stakes are big."

Newboy had learned how to bluff in backyard poker games in Bowling Green, Kentucky. And I remember thinking, "This is the poker game of your life. Don't let him read anything in your eyes, don't blink on him." The truth was that we were broke, we had no buyer, and we had to sell Guana to the State right now or the Ponte Vedra Inn and Club was gone.

We got up in that room, and he sat down with all of his notes in front of him. He was very organized. I just sat there and looked at him. The first thing he said was, and I'm sure he had instructions to come over here from Tallahassee to say this, "Now Mr. Peyton, the first thing I want you to know is that we know what you paid for all these assets." He said, "You paid $60 million."

Then he started reading off things that we had gotten for $60 million: Deerwood, Deerwood Center, Ponte Vedra Inn and Club, Guana, the four quadrants up at J. Turner Butler and Southside Boulevard, and other real estate around Jacksonville and around the southside of Jacksonville, and he got about halfway through the list. What he was leading to was that we hadn't paid much for Guana. But he didn't get that far. I said, "Wait just a damn minute. That's not what we're here to talk about. Now we've got our appraisal on Guana and you've got your appraisal on Guana."

And I said, "I know exactly what that island is worth, and if you people don't want it, that's fine, you go back to Tallahassee and there will be no hard feelings. If you do want it, the price is $53 million, because that is what it is appraised for. And there is no use talking about these other assets that haven't got a damn thing to do with it. And furthermore, I've got a developer who wants to buy that island, and I told him I'd call him in the morning and let him know. If you people don't want it, just tell me right now."

When I said that, the conversation stopped, and there

wasn't a sound in the room, and he didn't move a muscle.
He stared at me and I stared at him and I know it seemed
like five minutes, but it must have been two or three. And
I thought he was going to say, "You can go to hell. We're
not going to give you that kind of money for that island,"
and walk out. And I didn't flinch and he didn't. Finally, the
first thing he said was, "Okay, but let me ask you one thing.
I want to keep it under fifty million dollars because it
sounds so much better than fifty. I want to make it forty-
nine something." And I said, "That's fine." We shook
hands, and that was the deal.

If I had shown any weakness, or gone along with his
rationale about what we had paid for all the assets, the
whole thing would have caved in. I think that was really
the crossroads of my whole business career. And I think
Newboy's training, and standing up to the bullies at recess,
and Coach Donaldson telling us never to let them know
you're tired—I think all that paid off at that point.

Fortunately they didn't send a veteran negotiator like
John DeGrove over here. He might have said, "Peyton,
guess what. You may have a developer that you are going
to call in the morning, but when you call him you can also
tell him that he will get no permits to develop that island,
and I guarantee it will never be developed. I promise you
that." John was a man my age, he's tough, and he could
have pulled it off. Because the State really controlled that
island, because they control the permits.

The people who predicted that we would sell Ponte
Vedra within three months also said we didn't have the
ability to operate Ponte Vedra. To me and to Gate, Ponte
Vedra was a tremendous challenge; a challenge to see
whether service station operators were diverse enough to

operate a plush resort. Believe me, it was unlike managing Moncrief.

Ponte Vedra is 325 acres, almost a half mile on the Atlantic Ocean, and has been in operation for over sixty years. It is the best resort on the east coast of North America without any question, and one of the best in the country. We worked very hard on upgrading the staff and we take a great deal of pride in the ownership, and intend to keep improving.

The Gate people managed to make this transition and I think they did it successfully. When somebody comes up to me and says how much they like Ponte Vedra, what a great job we've done with the Club, and so forth, it gives me more pride than just about anything else. I am especially proud when the former SWD officers compliment me on Ponte Vedra, because I know they, along with many other people in Jacksonville, were very apprehensive when Gate Petroleum Company became the owners of Ponte Vedra.

Not long after we took ownership, we took a membership survey in which time and time again, members complained that employees and staff at Ponte Vedra were "surly." We made an all-out effort to eliminate that word from the Ponte Vedra vocabulary, and we never hear that word out there anymore.

When people come to Ponte Vedra, they expect to be treated politely and given service. That's exactly what they paid for, and when they don't get it, they get irate. We got many letters back from the survey, attached to the members' filled-out questionnaires. The membership had never been asked about Ponte Vedra matters before, and they had pent-up emotions about Ponte Vedra; the response was overwhelming.

I remember one lady said that she had been very upset when she heard that Gate Petroleum Company had bought Ponte Vedra, because she could envision good ole boys sitting around the fireplace and having "salesman of the month" meetings.

I go down there about four mornings a week, and either swim, run, or go through the Nautilus workout, take a steam bath, and go across the street for breakfast at the Inn. I go out there some for dinner. Of all the things we've been fortunate enough to get involved in, Ponte Vedra to me is still the most unbelievable. When I go there, I am still overwhelmed by its beauty and elegance.

Ponte Vedra is managed by Dale Haney with a staff of five hundred. These people are the best at what they do and take great pride in Ponte Vedra.

A few summers ago, Mother was at a cocktail party up in North Carolina and a lady came in a big car, diamonds hanging all over her, and obviously from high society. She started around the room introducing herself very flamboyantly, and said to Mother, "Where are you from, Mrs. Peyton?"

And Mother said, "I'm from Jacksonville." And the lady said, "Oh, how nice. My husband and I go down to spend a week at the Ponte Vedra Inn and Club every summer. Do you know where that is, Mrs. Peyton?" And Ma said, "Yes, as a matter of fact I do. My son owns it." She tells that story with great embellishment.

Mother sometimes has a funny way of looking at things. I went to see her one Sunday afternoon sometime after the SWD acquisition, and she said "Herby, you seem awfully quiet, is anything bothering you?" I said, "Yes, as a matter of fact, there is. We are now in debt to bankers over seventy-five million dollars and we are having a hard time and the bankers are unhappy." Her immediate response to this was, "That's not your fault. That's the bankers' fault. The bankers should never have loaned you the money in the first place." I take great delight in telling Billy Walker what my mother said.

In the late 1980s, the Japanese developed a strong desire to own golf course resorts, particularly on the ocean. They bought a lot of resorts around the country, the most famous of which was Pebble Beach in California. They decided they should own Ponte Vedra Inn and Club. During that period they made three passes at the Ponte Vedra Inn and Club. The first two came through brokers, and the last one was a phone call to me from Dallas, from a Japanese businessman. He said, "Mr. Pay-tahn, I want to fly over to Jacksonville from Dallas to talk to you about buying Ponte Vedra Inn and Club." And I told him that would be a waste of a plane ticket because Ponte Vedra was not for sale. And he replied that they were prepared to make a substantial cash offer for the Club. And I said, "Well that's fine, but it's not for sale." And he said, "Mr. Pay-tahn, are you telling me that Ponte Vedra is not for sale at any price?" And I said, " You got it. Sayonara." And he said "Goodbye," and that was the end of that.

Ponte Vedra is an institution and should be locally owned. And besides that, it just so happens that I am old enough to remember Pearl Harbor; therefore, Ponte Vedra will not be sold to the Japanese. I clearly remember when I was nine years old at Granny White Pike in Nashville, Tennessee, on Sunday, December 7, 1941. The whole family was huddled around that old roundtop Philco radio in the kitchen when the news came in. I also remember what Pa had to say about the "Japs," which will remain unsaid in this book.

It took us a quarter of a century to advance from Moncrief to Ponte Vedra. We are now entrenched. There will be no retreat.

— Chapter Sixteen —

Jacksonville – A Business City

Jacksonville lies twenty miles inland from some of Florida's most beautiful beaches. The U.S. Navy has a strong presence in Jacksonville with three bases, and it is common knowledge that most Navy personnel would rather be stationed in Jacksonville than in any other port, because this is a desirable place to live. Jacksonville's St. Johns River provides one of the finest deepwater ports on the nation's east coast.

Wide beaches, naval bases, and deepwater port—an impressive combination, yet these outstanding assets are not what Jacksonville is really all about. Jacksonville is about business. Jacksonville has always been and still is today, a good business town. Over the years we have produced more than our share of outstanding business leaders. Among them have been Ed Ball, J.E. Davis, and Raymond Mason.

First there was Ed Ball, who built a dynasty in Florida with the St. Joe Paper Company and Florida East Coast Railroad. Ed Ball's philosophy was very simple. He believed in accumulating assets and paying out as little as possible. He resented paying his help and his taxes. As a result, he paid his management people very little, and he avoided taxes by not showing profits.

For example, Florida East Coast was the first railroad in the country that used all concrete crossties. The purpose of investing in these expensive crossties was to hold down profits, thereby avoiding taxes. Mr. Ball accumulated over a million acres of Florida real estate. Very little of this real estate was sold during his lifetime, because the sale would involve paying taxes, and the way to handle that was not to sell real estate.

The finest businessman this city has ever produced, in my opinion, was J.E. Davis. J.E. was cofounder, with his brothers, of Winn Dixie, which is Jacksonville's leading company. J.E. was a master at providing the pure leadership required to put this company together. His specialty was controlling expenses.

J.E.'s particular genius was in numbers. He could analyze financial statements better than anyone else I have ever known. He had a photographic memory when it came to numbers. He could tell you what most major companies in the country made in the second or third quarter of last year. He could also tell you what their stock prices were, what their stock fluctuations were, and the culture of the particular company. He was an avid student of the stock market and a bigtime trader. He bought a stock for one purpose—that was for it to go up; if it didn't go up, he sold it. There was no emotion, it was pure numbers.

J.E. came from the old school; he believed in hard work. Most of his energy was devoted to the pursuit of business and profits. I used to visit him at his ranch in Montana in the summers, and he told me while we were rocking on the back porch late in the afternoon, on more than one occasion, that golf was a waste of time and football was a waste of energy. J.E. was an avid reader and had many interests. He loved the woods and wildlife, and had a particular interest in bears. He knew all about bears, and spent a great deal of time observing them in their natural habitat.

In 1989 the Berlin Wall came down and soon after, the Russian Empire came apart like a two-dollar watch, thereby ending the communist threat. At that time J.E. told me the stock market was going to do very well because the communist threat had hung over the free world for so long that it had stifled the world economy. With that threat now gone, he said the world would prosper. He was right as usual, and the strongest bull market in the history of this country has occurred since the fall of the Iron Curtain.

Perhaps J.E.'s finest hour was when he single-handedly convinced Mayo Clinic to build their first-ever branch in Jacksonville. It did not happen, however, in an hour. It took years of persuading and pressure as only he could do. He finally just wore them out.

J.E. was a classic philanthropist, and contributed more to Jacksonville than has anyone else, before or since. This business giant died in the spring of 1993, and Jacksonville will never see the likes of him again.

Raymond Mason built the Charter Oil Company from scratch. This New York Stock Exchange company was a true conglomerate, headquartered in Jacksonville. Raymond Mason is one of the few men in the history of this country that had, in one year, a profit of $1 million a day after taxes—$365 million. Charter wound up bankrupt, which meant that he lost profits plus several hundred million additional dollars.

Many years ago, a lawyer friend of mine went to work for Charter. He joined the company at a top management position. He went to his first board meeting and heard various managers explain the graphs which filled the wall. He sat quiet and still. My friend noticed the graph of one particular operation that was losing money every month, except that about nine months into the future the graph started up at about a forty-five degree angle showing the sales and profits improving dynamically. My friend opened his mouth for the first time and asked, "Would someone explain to me why this company, after nine months of projected losses, would all of a sudden experience this tremendous turnaround?" A hush fell over the room, and all motion ceased. At that time, Raymond Mason leaned over, put his hand on my friend's forearm, and said in almost a whisper, "Now, let's don't be pessimistic."

The always optimistic Raymond Mason was a master at acquisitions, but after he acquired a company, he was not a master at managing people, and that eventually was Charter's downfall. Still, his acquisition skills continue to be unsurpassed in this city.

These men, along with others, each in their own special way, have built one of the premier business cities of the Southeast—Jacksonville.

Chapter Seventeen

River Trouble

All of my life I have been fascinated by rivers. Over the years, I have had the pleasure of going down some of the most beautiful rivers in North America, preferably by canoe. I have learned that when trouble comes on the river, it usually comes very suddenly and can be some of Mother Nature's most vicious behavior.

About six years ago, J. E. Davis invited me to visit at his Okaga Ranch in northwest Montana. I have always loved the West, but to me, Montana was a cut above all the other western states. Montana is like Colorado except bigger and better, with fewer people. I remember on my first visit to J.E.'s ranch, my wife, Murph, and I were jogging down a gravel road early one morning and a big brown bear came out of the woods and stopped, squinted at us and sniffed the air several times. We stopped running and froze in our tracks. For a brief period we didn't know whether he was going to come after us or continue to cross the road. He decided to continue across the road and Murph decided that was the last time she would go jogging in Montana.

It has been nearly two hundred years since Lewis and Clark made their much-heralded journey across the Northwest to unlock the West for an aggressive young nation. Over one-quarter of this trip took place in Montana and much of what they saw remains unchanged.

Montana is laced with beautiful and remote rivers. You can sometimes go a hundred miles on these rivers and never see a person. About five years ago I decided the time had come for me to do some serious canoeing in Montana. I bought an aluminum canoe and left it at J.E.'s ranch, and returned for three summers to make a canoe trip on a different river each time. I recruited Hill, my middle son, who is now in his mid-twenties, to accompany me on these adventures. I discovered early that Hill was big and strong and not only could paddle a canoe all day long and portage it around the rapids, but could lift me out of the river by the nape of the neck when I was thrown overboard.

The first year we put in on the Yakk River near J.E.'s ranch and proceeded south. We had a good trip that went well until the afternoon of the second day. We were in extremely swift rapids and the canoe got lodged on a large rock just under the surface and turned sideways. Pinned there by the current, the canoe filled up with water and dumped us in the raging river. We managed to get to shore and walk out to a hard road. Eventually with the help of a forest ranger we recovered our canoe and had it transported back to J.E.'s ranch.

The next summer we attacked the Kootennai River. This river is also in northwest Montana and it runs west into Idaho and then north to the Canadian border. Pushing off into the rapids, that first day, I told Hill that we had a hundred miles to go and there wasn't but one way to get there. And that was to paddle. He commenced paddling in earnest. During our three-day period we were in true wilderness and except for people in the one small town we passed through, we never saw a boat or a person on the river. The trip was very physical because we not only had some rapids but also had some dead water which meant paddling hard all day. At one point we had to drag the canoe and carry our equipment for more that a quarter of a mile. We also had some rainstorms, high winds and cold, and when we finally got to the Canadian border we were totally exhausted and could barely get out of the canoe and walk upright.

My third river trip in Montana was in the summer of 1996. Hill got out of the notion and I recruited my oldest son, John, who is in his early thirties, for this mission. I called the Kalispell, Montana, Chamber of Commerce for their advice. They referred me to the Fish, Wildlife and Parks Service for the State of Montana. I called out there and talked to a man named Murle Phillips. I told Murle that I was looking for a river that had at least a hundred miles of swift rapids in a remote area with no people. He said, "I know just the place. You need to fly to Kalispell and I will take you north to the Canadian border and you can come down the north fork of the Flathead River."

He warned that this river was very swift and we should not attempt it unless we were expert canoeists. I thanked him and told him that we would be there in the last half of June. I also gave him my phone number.

About a week before John and I were to depart for Montana, Murle called and advised me not to come until later in the summer. A late spring had resulted in the glaciers melting late. The river was high and very dangerous, made worse by heavy rains. I told him that we already had our plane tickets and had arranged to get off work, and that my son and I would be there in about a week.

I arranged for my canoe to be transported from J.E.'s ranch to Murle Phillips' place in Kalispell, about a hundred miles. When John and I arrived we had our canoe and the best of equipment. We had all of our equipment and food in tough waterproof bags. Everything was to be strapped into the canoe with bungee cords. We had a North Face tent, sleeping bags, .757 magnum Colt pistol, ax, flashlight, knife, lifejackets, bicycle helmets, alcohol stove, spare paddle, bailer made from a gallon plastic milk jug, and several changes of clothes. The food consisted of tuna fish, sardines, Nabs, crackers, fruit cocktail, juices, and cereal with a special kind of milk that did not have to be refrigerated. For evening meals, we had precooked, packaged meals that we put in boiling water. Some of these supplies were added in Kalispell, and we were ready to go.

Murle was extremely nice to us, transported us all around the town, and took us to meet the main forest ranger in that area. Murle, John, the forest ranger and I had a long talk that morning. The forest ranger warned us we were going into the heart of bear country and that we should have our pistol ready at all times. He also said that the moose were more aggressive than bears and would attack us if they could get to us.

The ranger advised us that we should not go on the Flathead River in a canoe but should go in a rubber raft, because with the high water, the river was treacherous and very unforgiving. He said the rapids were tough but the biggest danger was in the logjams. He talked in the language of the river and explained to us about what they called a sweeper—a tree that has fallen over into the river with its root system intact at the bank. The sweeper accumulates logs floating down the river, forming a logjam. He told us that if we got caught in the logjam we would be sucked under and drowned. He explained that there was an unusual number of logjams this spring because the high water had eroded the banks and the trees closest to the banks had fallen into the river at many places. He also explained that the river frequently braids as it heads south, which meant there would be two and three forks, and sometimes even four, where the current would weave in and out. He told us we should always choose the biggest braid because it would be least apt to be stopped up with logjams.

He also told us that the forest service monitors this river year round. The water level was now three feet higher than normal and the water temperature was 38 degrees—six degrees above freezing. He concluded by telling us that if we got in the water, we would not last long.

When Murle, John and I left our forest ranger friend after his very sobering talk, John said, "Well look, if we can make the same trip in a raft instead of in a canoe, and eliminate the risk, that is the sensible thing to do." I told John over dinner that night and breakfast early the next morning that there was nothing on that river we couldn't handle in a canoe. He finally reluctantly agreed.

The next morning we loaded our canoe on Murle's pickup truck and the three of us headed north a hundred miles to the Canadian border. We had decided to drop off our rented Explorer at the halfway point, where Big Creek dumps into the Flathead River. We wanted the Explorer left there for two reasons: one was if we got in trouble, we'd have a way out. The other was that we could lighten the canoe for the last part of the trip by leaving some of our supplies in the Explorer.

The elevation of Kalispell is near 3,000 feet and after you climb up to the Canadian border you're at about 5,000 feet. It was late morning when we finally bade farewell to Murle and pushed off in the canoe. That afternoon we literally flew down the river. The current was between ten and twelve miles an hour and the force of the water was unbelievable. Although we took on water several times and stopped to bail out the canoe, we made good time and camped on the riverbank late that afternoon.

Our campsite was great. We were on lush green grass on a bluff overlooking the river. The canoe was turned upside down by the tent, and as we looked to the east, we could see the western rim of the Continental Divide and the glaciers we had heard so much about. These snowcapped mountains must have been twenty or thirty miles away, but the air was so clear it looked like we could almost touch them. It was extremely quiet except for the rustling sound of the river.

After supper, John went down to wash off pans in the river. When he came back up to the campsite he said his hands were aching because the water was so frigid. That night it got very cold. When I got up the next morning, I thought there was frost on the canoe. I went over and looked more closely and discovered it was not frost, but ice. We built a fire, warmed up, ate breakfast, waited for the sun to warm things up, and shoved off about nine o'clock.

Again, the water quickly moved us down the river. Just before noon we stopped and took a long break—had tuna fish, crackers and juice and even sprawled out on the grass and took a short nap. In early afternoon we took off down the river again. We were wearing our bicycle helmets and lifejackets and had all our equipment strapped into the canoe.

We had paddled about an hour and a half or two hours when we came around this bend and the river was braided with three forks. I was in the front of the canoe and told John we should take the right fork. As we approached the right fork John said the middle fork looked bigger and better and we should change over to the middle fork. I said "Okay, let's go!" and we swung the bow of the canoe to the left to get into the middle fork. We were both paddling as hard as we could and thought we would have no trouble switching to the middle fork, but there was a logjam at the head of that fork.

I thought we had cleared the logjam and the front half of the canoe did, but the back half hit the logs and the force of the water caused the back gunwale to dip, and the canoe filled with water. It then turned over. As it took off down the river it made creaking, groaning noises like a sinking ship.

All this happened in a matter of seconds, and I can remember thinking, "This can't be happening." John was thrown from the canoe and disappeared under the logjam. I hung onto the canoe and I was carried down the river for about fifty yards. The canoe crashed into another logjam and I found myself mashed between the canoe and a log. I managed to let go of the canoe and hold onto the log. The canoe went around the log and proceeded down the river.

The log that I was holding onto was a sweeper. I found myself wrapped around the log with my shoulders and head above the log and my body from my chest down pulled and pinned under the log by the current. I held onto the log for dear life. I looked over my shoulder for John and he was nowhere to be seen. I was terrified that he had drowned after he had been sucked under the first logjam.

I hung onto the log and tried to get my breath. Though it must have been only three to five minutes it seemed much longer as I looked desperately over my shoulder for John.

All of a sudden, John didn't just come up, he popped up out of the water like a cork, his lifejacket holding him up. I waved and screamed at him. The current brought him down to me very fast and we were soon both holding onto the same log for life.

John said when he was thrown from the canoe, he had held onto the log we had struck. The current had filled his loose-fitting bicycle helmet with water holding his head under. Before complete exhaustion set in he had been able to pull his head up several times gasping for breath. His lungs had begun filling with water. He had finally given up and let go, thinking he was drowning. When he had let go, the current had taken him under the logjam and he had bobbed up on the downstream side.

When John arrived next to me at the log he was totally exhausted. I was so encouraged and relieved by John's arrival that I found the strength to pull one leg over the log, and eventually to drag my whole body up out of the current and onto the log. I reached down and told John to give me his hand. He said no, he was afraid to let go. I eventually grabbed him under the armpits and pulled him onto the log, and we climbed to shore. We then conducted a brief search for the canoe and determined that it was gone.

We both knew that we were still in serious trouble, because we were on an island in the middle of a wild river. We began slogging across the island to determine where best to swim the river. The island was about a mile long and a quarter of a mile wide. As we crossed the island we waded through hip-deep creeks and sloughs. John asked me if they had quicksand up there, and I told him I didn't know, but we were going to find out.

We ran across fresh moose tracks which we could tell had just been made. While we were in Kalispell buying our supplies, we had bought a whistle for the purpose of scaring off bears, moose or whatever, and John had it clipped to his lifejacket. I told him to blow the whistle as we found our way across the island.

When we finally got to the bank of the island, we had to walk up the river to choose the best place to swim across. At this point John was reluctant and said we should continue to look for a better place. I told him that we'd have to swim the river and we had to swim it now, because we were running out of time. The first signs of hypothermia were beginning to show. We had been operating on pure adrenaline.

We picked a spot to cross the river where there were no sweepers on the other side, so that when we got across we would not be sucked under another logjam. The river was about forty yards wide and the current was ripping. We waded out as far as we could go and started swimming. John was right next to me. He was gasping for air like he was drowning and it scared me. The current shoved my bicycle helmet over my eyes. I couldn't raise my head to breathe and I couldn't see where I was going so I stopped, treaded water, took off the helmet and let it go. While I was stopped, John got out ahead of me, got caught in the current and washed downstream.

John finally got to the other bank but because of some bushes, he couldn't see me. When he saw my helmet floating down the river, he thought I was under the helmet and had drowned. He got up on the bank and chased the helmet, calling out for me. Meanwhile, I finally got across the river and found myself at the bottom of a bluff. I eventually got hold of a root about as big as my arm and muscled my way up the bank. When I stood up, away from the roar of the river, I could hear John yelling "Dad!" I answered and after several exchanges of calls we got back together.

By the time we got together, John was near delirium. I noticed his eyes had a strange glaze and he was disoriented. Hypothermia had moved in. He didn't know which direction to go, and wanted to follow the river. I insisted that he walk behind me and we would walk due west, because I remembered from reading the maps there was a road west of the river. I told him to continue blowing the whistle, and we took off through a heavily wooded area. As the terrain started to rise the woods got thinner, and after about a mile and a half we came out on a gravel road. By this time we had been in and out of icy water for close to an hour. I told John that we were going to walk on that road as fast as we could and we were not going to stop or slow down and we were going to go to Big Creek, where our Explorer was stashed. We figured that Big Creek was about fifteen miles down that road.

We walked at top speed for about a mile, and then we heard a truck coming down the road. The driver was an old bearded man who was heading south, the direction we wanted to go. We started thumbing for a ride but it was obvious to me the driver wasn't going to stop, so I stood in the middle of the road and waved both arms. He slid to a stop. I told him we were in trouble and needed a ride to Big Creek. He said he had no room in the cab and there was garbage in the back. I said "That's fine"; we hopped on the garbage and he took off.

When we got to Big Creek he let us out and we thanked him. By this time hypothermia had come in earnest. Both of us started, at about the same time, this violent shivering almost like we were in convulsions. We managed to get into the Explorer and turn on the heater. We couldn't drive because of the shivering, but we sat there for about thirty minutes and warmed up. Then we drove back to Kalispell.

John and I checked into the motel, took a long hot shower, and invited Murle Phillips over to dinner. When we told Murle what had happened, he told us we were lucky to be alive. Then he shared some western wisdom with us. That was, "When you get right down to it, a man is very hard to kill, and to actually kill one, you've got to step on him like a cockroach or he will somehow survive."

The forest rangers and Murle searched the river for the canoe but to no avail. Two and a half weeks later, Murle called me at home, advised me that the water level had dropped and they had found the canoe. It evidently had been trapped under a logjam. The logs had shifted and the bow was sticking straight up out of the river about three feet. The waterproof bags were still intact and he was able to recover most of our equipment and ship it to us. He told us the canoe was twisted, banged-up and a total loss.

We had escaped the icy jaws of the Flathead River with abrasions, bruises, hypothermia, and total exhaustion. I was tremendously impressed with the way John had conducted himself. He remained calm, and we both went about doing what we knew we had to do. Looking back on our ordeal, I realized some strange things had happened. Perhaps the strangest was that although the water was six degrees above freezing, neither one of us had felt the cold of the water because we were operating on pure adrenaline. Evidently, when we hit the water, all of our blood retreated into the cores of our bodies and adrenaline took over. Our minds were racing and our physical strength was unbelievable. I noticed when we were walking across the island that my mouth was dry and I was frequently spitting and the taste of brass was present.

Another strange thing that happened concerned a deep gash on my left shin from the log. When we got back to town, I noticed the cut but thought it was little more than a scratch because it had not bled. Days later, I realized that it was a deep cut to the bone. In fact, my shin took several months to heal and is still scarred. I then realized that it had not bled because of the cold water and the flow of adrenaline.

After a couple of days in Kalispell, John and I flew back to Jacksonville, and we arrived at the Jacksonville airport at midnight. Hill met us at the airport. John had circles under his eyes, had lost weight, and looked very weary. As we walked down the airport concourse, I heard Hill tell John in a very low voice, "I tried to tell you!"

Some time after arriving back in Jacksonville, I realized that the teachings of the Flathead River had changed my life forever. I had discovered there is no horror in this world like thinking you have been responsible for the death of your son. The most terrifying event in my life was the few minutes when John disappeared in the river.

My priorities have totally changed. I now understand that things which used to bother me, such as running late to a meeting, traffic jams, the dog days of later summer in Florida, and the normal frustrations of business, don't matter.

I had the luck of the draw to be born in America. I am indeed fortunate to enjoy good health because I have had strained milk all my life. Along the way I have had more than a dozen broken bones, often as a result of doing things I had no business doing in the first place.

I love and appreciate my family much more than before. When I go home at night and my two-year-old daughter, Sarah, comes running down the hall and says, "Hi, Dada," my day is complete. And when my five-year-old son,

Forest, asks me to play football with him, I am excited and ready to go.

In my opinion, the true test of any family is the transition of a business from one generation to the next. I am very fortunate to have two sons, John and Hill, with the company. They have both worked hard and are good at what they do. The transition of the company to them and to the next generation of Gate brothers is now in progress, and I am sure they will do better than we ever did.

My daughter, Gaines, who has inherited her artistic ability from my mother, is an excellent artist with a great future and is currently the director of an art gallery in New York City. The family is very proud of her.

My whole life is centered around Murph, my wife of seven years, whom I love very much and who is my best friend. Her teenage daughter Alyssa, lives with us at Rivergate and has become very special to me.

Mother lives in Epping Forest and is now a hundred years old. She still tells us that Sister is remarkable. Sister and her husband live in Jacksonville. Brother is retired now and lives in Charleston, South Carolina. He doesn't ride freight trains anymore, and has long ago discarded his traps. But he still does go fishing every chance he gets. When Brother comes to see Mother, we all get together and talk about the long ago days in Kentucky.

—Chapter Eighteen—

The Storm

J acksonville was just a sleepy port town of about 130 thousand back in the 1930s. It went through the depression and got hurt like everybody got hurt. Then there was some growth, but not really dynamic growth, and after World War II the city was controlled by a group of wealthy families, concentrated in Ortega. They were very smug, and most of them feared that we'd go right back into depression after World War II, so they were not willing to put out any seed money for anything. As a result, the city did not really grow as it should have. And yet the Ortegans had control over almost everything in Jacksonville that was worth anything.

As recently as the mid-seventies, the talk around the state was that Jacksonville was just a stagnant, south Georgia port town, and that its progress really couldn't be compared with the growth of the rest of Florida. By any standard of comparison, its growth never did keep pace.

The reason for that was the local power base. Jacksonville, like other cities, has its exclusive neighborhood address synonymous with wealth. Ortega, on the west side of the St. Johns River, graces an oak-shaded point where the Ortega River flows into the St. Johns. From Ortega's manicured lawns, the city skyline seems to rise like Atlantis across the river to the north.

When Gate's takeovers continued with Houdaille-Duval, Southpoint, and even Stockton Whatley Davin's Real Estate Division, it was somewhat amusing to the Old

Boys. But then in a short period of time we added Epping Forest and Blount Island, and it was no longer funny. They realized that Jacksonville had changed, and they had lost control of the city. They hadn't intended for this to happen, and there's some resentment in Jacksonville even today.

The Old Boys had allowed Newboy to come out of nowhere and take away over half a billion dollars worth of the prime assets of this town while they shied away from risking capital. They hadn't seen it coming at all, because Newboy was not one of them. It was inevitable that as Jacksonville grew and prospered, the Ortegans could not continue to control the city's power base. They had expected the ownership of Duval County to shift among themselves, but not to an outsider, certainly not to Newboy.

Not Newboy, who throughout his school days, was chosen last at recess and sat nameless on the back row. Not to Newboy, who came to Jacksonville via the Mississippi River on a homemade raft. Not to Newboy, who was a private in the army and never even got to go to war. Not to Newboy, who was beaten up, shot at, and robbed, at Moncrief. Not to Newboy, of whom Biggie has said many times, "I can hold my breath longer than Peyton stayed at the University of Florida."

The only time I get invited to Ortega is for fundraisers, and when I get over there, they are interested in two things: how much can I give, and when? I somehow don't feel very comfortable over there, but then I'm not sure they would feel very comfortable in the backyard of 1220 State Street in Bowling Green, or for that matter, at Moncrief.

In the fall of 1962, I bought eight acres on the St. Johns River in Mandarin and lived in a Jim Walters house on the property. When I moved there, an old frame house built before the Civil War was still standing, although not livable. After many years, when I got able, I tore down the old house and the Jim Walters house and built my new home, Rivergate, on this site. In the facing of the fireplace below the mantel, I have four bricks, over one hundred years old, from the chimney of the frame house, and four bricks from the Ponte Vedra.

I told my children two things I hoped they would never do in their lifetimes: one would be to sell our home, Rivergate; and the other would be to give up ownership of Ponte Vedra Inn and Club. The eight bricks in our mantel are to remind them of this request.

When the battle of the acquisitions was over, it was apparent that the Old Guard had lost their stranglehold on Jacksonville to Newboy, and the River City would never be the same. After the smoke of battle had cleared, I was at Rivergate late one hot afternoon. I walked out to the end of my dock to watch a summer thunderstorm rumbling in from the northwest.

Massive black storm clouds were boiling up over Ortega, driving silver sheets of rain ahead of them as the front crossed the river toward Mandarin. Cooled air rushed over me as I watched the rain racing nearer, and I thought how perfectly nature was mirroring the dispersal of Jacksonville's old power base by the winds of change.

As rain darkened the weathered boards of my lonely dock, and the first big drops splattered on my face, I noticed something strange about the rain. It tasted salty. I realized I was crying a lifetime of unshed tears. Newboy training was over.

Gate Brothers & Sisters

These are the people who built Gate Petroleum Company.

Gail Adams

Charles E. Adcock, Jr.

Carolyn Aikens

Pete Akers (2)

A. C. Ball (1) (5)

Harold Berryhill (4)

Ann Bishop

Gerry Boyer

James Peter Britt (1) (5)

Fred N. Brown

John B. Burnette

Williard Callahan (2)

Barbara Campbell (2) (5)

John Campbell (2)

Jim Citrano

Benny Cleghorn (2)

Theresa Clements

Annette Colgrove

Martha Copeland

Darlene Cowen

Donald R. Davis (3)

Henry Davis (2)

Ray Day (2)

David Dill

Dawn Eggleston

Charles Everington (2)

Billy Flowers

Ray Gallivan

John Gibson

Pam Gibson

Marlene C. Giese (1)

Donald Gilliam

Thomas M. Glavin

Jerry K. Green

Karen Greene

Pat Grey

Brenda Guyton

Frank Gwaltney

William V. Gwin

Diane Hall

Dale Haney (3)

Murle Harrison (3)

Lydia Hazen (2)

Robert F. Hoefer

Jim Holdman

Robert B. Hoover

Alan P. Hudgins

Rodney Hutson

Billy Jenkins, Sr.

Jay Johnson

Jim Johnson

Ken Johnson (4)

Melody Johnson

Ronald Johnston

Brenda P. Jones

Michael L. Junk

Ron Kalapp (2)

Ted Kilpatrick (4)

Wayne M. Levitt (1)

Dizzie D. Locklear (1) (4)

Robbie Loggins

Mike Love

Jack C. Lueders, Jr.
Joseph C. Luke
Ernest Manning (1) (4)
Thomas A. Mantia
Russell T. Matheny (1) (5)
John Mather
Bobby W. Mathis, Sr. (1) (5)
Bobby W. Mathis, Jr.
James E. McCormack
Neil Z. McEachern (4)
Albert McLain
Jack McMahon (2) (5)
John McMahon
Johnny McManus
Betty Miller
Zdravko Mincek (3)
Frank Mitchell
Robert R. Moody (1)
Don Moore
Jose Morales
Susan Morgan
George E. Nail
Rita Palmer
Shirley M. Patten
Henry Hill Petyon
John Stephens Peyton
Albert S. Phillips
Donna Ponder
Sammy Potts (1) (4)
Carl A. Register
Mitchell Rhodes
Billy Rhodes (1) (5)
John Ricker
Kim Ricker
Worth Riggins
James R. Russ

Pete Scowcroft (2)
Margaret Sikes
P. Jeremy Smith, Jr.
Bill Spencer (2) (4)
Jim Stickler
Sharon Stoops
Jim Taylor
Thomas N. Thurson
Jack Urso
Leo Van Dyke (2)
Tommy R. Vasser, Jr.
Nathan Walker (4)
Wilbert Walker
Russell F. Walthour
John Walton
Don Watson
Howard B. Weadon
Robert A. Westendick
Kathleen Williams
Kenneth P. Wilson (3)
R. L. Wimburn
Ernest L. Winney
Mary Woodley
Dean Yeager
Louis M. Zemanek (1)

(1) Former Billups Employee

(2) Former Houdaille-Duval Employee

(3) Former Stockton, Whatley, Davin Employee

(4) Retired

(5) Deceased

Glossary of Terms

Belly wash— Coca-Cola or other soft drinks

Black as Egypt — dark night

Bloodsuckers — major oil companies

Break from sucking eggs—breaking a bad habit

Burning daylight — sleeping after daybreak

Clean your plough — leave you broke

Come apart like a two-dollar watch — come unwelded

Come unwelded — come apart under pressure

Crazy as a bat — thoroughly demented

Cutthroats — independent stations that do not sell a major brand

Feet wore off up to your knees — condition brought on by long standing on service station driveway

Get a new hustle — diversify

Getting out of the notion— changing ones mind

Grappling — a method of fishing in Tennessee and Kentucky in which you reach under rocks to catch fish — or whatever else is under there

Hates it like the devil hates holy water — dislikes it in the extreme

Hawk on a June bug — pursue someone aggressively

Holding nothing but the Ten Commandments — broke

Laying up — sleeping late in morning

Like crows on a limb — people with similar looks

Moneychangers — bankers

Pissant — to carry, as do certain Kentucky ants which always carry large loads

Portage — carrying a canoe around impassable rapids

Possum — one who works in a service station

Rich as six foot up a bull's ass — very wealthy

Scared my mule — frightened me into at least considering running like hell

Self-tackleization — a mishap or disaster brought about by one's own error

Sick as a yard dog — nauseated

Slow as smoke — person who moves slowly

Snake bit — cursed with ongoing bad luck and made cautious by the experience

Straightleg — any soldier in the Army who does not jump out of airplanes

Strained milk — physically and mentally stressed

The bear's got you — you have passed out from exhaustion

Traipsin'—wandering

Triflin' — lazy, as in "no 'count"

Useless as tits on a boar hog — totally inept person

Working from can to can't —working from before daylight until after dark

Worriation — excessive worrying

Wouldn't give a nickel to see a pissant eat a bale of hay — description of a stingy person

Index

A

Aberley, Bill - 168, 170, 177

AETNA - 146

American General Corporation - 159

Arnold, Walter - 116, 117, 120, 158

Atlantic Bank - 175, 176,180

B

Bailey, Cecil - 114, 115

Ball, Ed - 194

Barker, Gini - ix

Barnett Bank - 110, 142, 146, 148, 162, 163, 183

Beard, Ralph - 32

Beckett, Welton - 159

BellSouth - 146

Bettersworth, Jay - 40, 69

Bigtree Racquet Club - 143

Billups Petroleum Company - 21, 62, 84, 85, 87, 97, 98, 105, 107, 110, 111

Bilyeu, Bobby - 32

Blue Cross & Blue Shield of FL. - 146

Bonnell, Gene - 167, 177, 178

Brant, Ish - 56

Brown, Ed - 176

Burns, Bill - 148

Burpee, Leland - 169

C

C&S Bank - 177, 180

Charter Oil Company - 153, 154, 196, 197

Ches Wyman Company - 2

Chestnut, James - 40, 48

Citrano, Jim - 111, 159, 214

Clark Family - 18, 19

Clark, O. V. - 18, 19

Clavier, Dave - ix

Cleghorn, Benny - 150, 214

Coach Campbell - 68

Collins, Oliver William (Uncle Bill) - 107, 108, 109, 164

Cooper, Dr. Ken - 57

Cowan, Darlene - 119

Culverhouse, Hugh - 171

Cushman Wakefield - 156

D

Davenport, Bobo - 32, 33

Davis, Don - 111

Davis, J.E. - 194, 195, 196, 198, 199, 200